MORE GREAT GAMES
FOR GROUPS

Zondervan/Youth Specialties Books

Professional Resources

Advanced Peer Counseling in Youth Groups
Called to Care
The Church and the American Teenager
   (*previously released as* Growing Up in America)
Developing Student Leaders
Feeding Your Forgotten Soul
Great Fundraising Ideas for Youth Groups
Help! I'm a Volunteer Youth Worker!
High School Ministry
How to Recruit and Train Volunteer Youth Workers
   (*previously released as* Unsung Heroes)
Junior High Ministry (Revised Edition)
The Ministry of Nurture
Organizing Your Youth Ministry
Peer Counseling in Youth Groups
Road Trip
The Youth Minister's Survival Guide
Youth Ministry Nuts and Bolts
The Youth Workers Promo Kit

Discussion Starter Resources

Amazing Tension Getters
Get 'Em Talking
High School TalkSheets
Hot Talks
Junior High TalkSheets
More High School TalkSheets
More Junior High TalkSheets
Option Plays
Parent Ministry TalkSheets
Teach 'Toons
Tension Getters
Tension Getters Two

Special Needs and Issues

The Complete Student Missions Handbook
Divorce Recovery for Teenagers
Ideas for Social Action
Intensive Care: Helping Teenagers in Crisis
Rock Talk
Teaching the Truth about Sex
Up Close and Personal: How to Build Community
   in Your Youth Group

Youth Ministry Programming

Adventure Games
Creative Programming Ideas for Junior High Ministry
Creative Socials and Special Events

Good Clean Fun
Good Clean Fun, Volume 2
Great Games for City Kids
Great Ideas for Small Youth Groups
Greatest Skits on Earth
Greatest Skits on Earth, Volume 2
Holiday Ideas for Youth Groups (Revised Edition)
Junior High Game Nights
More Junior High Game Nights
On-Site: 40 On-Location Youth Programs
Play It! Great Games for Groups
Play It Again! More Great Games for Groups
Super Sketches for Youth Ministry
Teaching the Bible Creatively
The Youth Specialties Handbook for
   Great Camps and Retreats

4th-6th Grade Ministry

Attention Grabbers for 4th-6th Graders
4th-6th Grade TalkSheets
Great Games for 4th-6th Graders
How to Survive Middle School
Incredible Stories
More Attention Grabbers for 4th-6th Graders
More Great Games for 4th-6th Graders
More Quick and Easy Activities for 4th-6th Graders
Quick and Easy Activities for 4th-6th Graders
Teach 'Toons

Clip Art

ArtSource™ Volume 1—Fantastic Activities
ArtSource™ Volume 2—Borders, Symbols,
   Holidays, and Attention Getters
ArtSource™ Volume 3—Sports
ArtSource™ Volume 4—Phrases and Verses
ArtSource™ Volume 5—Amazing Oddities and
   Appalling Images
ArtSource™ Volume 6—Spiritual Topics
Youth Specialties Clip Art Book
Youth Specialties Clip Art Book, Volume 2

Video

Next Time I Fall in Love Video Curriculum
Understanding Your Teenager Video Curriculum
Video Spots for Junior High Game Nights

Student Books

Going the Distance
Grow for It Journal
Next Time I Fall in Love
Next Time I Fall in Love Journal

MORE GREAT GAMES FOR GROUPS

WAYNE RICE

MIKE YACONELLI

Youth Specialties

ZondervanPublishingHouse
A Division of HarperCollinsPublishers

Play It Again!
Copyright ©1993 by Youth Specialties, Inc.

Youth Specialties Books, 1224 Greenfield Drive, El Cajon, California 92021,
are published by Zondervan Publishing House,
Grand Rapids, Michigan 49530

Library of Congress Cataloging in Publication Data

Play it again! : more great games for groups / Wayne Rice and Mike
      Yaconelli, editors.
            p.   cm.
      "Youth Specialties."
      Includes index.
      ISBN 0-310-37291-7
      1. Group games.   2. Cooperativeness.   I. Rice, Wayne.
II. Yaconelli, Mike.
GV1201.P53   1993
790. 1' 5--dc20   92-42833
                                                                          CIP

Edited by J. Cheri McLaughlin
Cover and interior design by PAZ Design Group

Printed in the United States of America
      94 95 96 97 98 99 / CH / 10 9 8 7 6 5 4 3

The games in *Play It Again!* originally appeared in the Ideas Library, published by Youth Specialties, Inc., and they are reprinted by permission.

The authors wish to thank all of the creative youth workers listed below who developed these games and who contributed them for publication. Without them, this book would not have been possible.

Mark Adams
Bill Aldridge
Julie Anderson
Daniel Atwood
Tommy Baker
Timothy Bean
June Becker
Jim Bell
Paul Bertelson
Phil Blackwell
Mark Boughan
Jay Brady
Steve Bridges
E. Parke Brown
Rick Brown
Kevin Bueltmann
Mark Byers
Jeff Callen
Michael W. Capps
Brian Cheek
Mark Christian
Jeffery Collins
Elliott Cooke
Rich Cooper
Randy Cooney
Keith Curran
Deborah Cusson
Len Cuthbert
John Davis
Laurie Delgatto
Len DiCicco
Brad Edgbert
Vernon Edington
Sondra Edwards

Glenn Embree
Scott Eynon
Rauel Feldhelzer
Terry Fisher
Pete Franzone
Michael Frisbee
Brian Fullerton
Tim Gerarden
Dick Gibson
John Gilbert
Christopher Graham
Thud Gudnason
Ralph Gustafson
Roger Haas
Mark A. Hahlen
Dave Hall
Joe Harvey
Randy Hausler
Jack Hawkins
Chris Hayes
Mick Hernandez
R. P. Hodge
Paul Holmberg
David Holton
Tom Jackson
Jim Johnson
Bert Jones
Pete Kenow
David Killinger
Keith King
Jeff Koch
John Krienke
John Krueger
Todd Ladd

Dick Lapine
Jim Larsen
John K. Larson
Terry Linhart
Philip Lopez
James Lutes
Tom Lytle
Sean Mahar
Dave Mahoney
Rob Marin
Ed Martinez
Tim Maughan
John McLendon
Jerry Meadows
Greg Miller
Jeff Minor
Chris Moore
Merle Moser, Jr.
Lisa Nyman
Scott Oas
Doug Partin
Barry Perkins
Keith Posehn
Lynn H. Pryor
Phil Rankin
David Rasmussen
Alan Rathbun
Jim Reed
James A. Rivers
Steve Robertson
Todd Rodarmel
Roger Rome
Steve Sayer
Mark Schwartz

Dale Shackley
David Shaw
David Sherwood
Mark Simone
Ann Smith
Bruce Smith
David Smith
Larry Smith
Steve Smoker
Gene Stable
Valerie Stoop
Lee Strawhun
John Stumbo
Fred Swallow
Gary Tapley
Chris Thompson
Carly Toews
Kevin Turner
Vaughn Van Skiver
Lyn Wargny
David Washburn
Ed Weaver
Rick Wheeler
Vernal Wilkinson
Bill Williamson
Brett Wilson
Ray Wilson
Andrew Winters
Fay Wong
John Yarnell
Mark Ziehr
Neil Zobel

T A B L E   O F
C O N T E N T S

C H A P T E R   1

INTRODUCTION

This is no ordinary game book. *Play It Again!* is our second collection of great group games that people—all kinds of people—will want to play.[1] This may sound surprising in a society where game playing has become something you watch—where a game is a highly competitive battle in which winning is everything and people don't matter. We believe, however, that people want to play games again and want to have fun.

In writing *Play It Again!* we chose only games with potential for community building, using specific criteria that have nothing to do with winning or with skill. These games are not only fun but are also playable by nearly everyone. They are occasions for celebration, not warfare.

Not that competition is inherently evil. Competition is useful when it increases the enjoyment of those who are playing. Good games are competitive; but competition is a detriment to game playing when it drives a wedge between the "good" and the "bad" players or the "skilled" and the "nonskilled." Winning should be either irrelevant or anticlimactic, never the focus of game playing.

Just as enjoyment is more important than competition, participation is more important than performance. Yet many of us, fearing ridicule or embarrassment, seem reluctant to participate actively in a game. We think we're not good enough, so we willingly accept the role of spectator. As a result, games have become the private domain of the athlete and the professional. But games were made to be played, not watched. It's time we reclaimed game playing for all of us, to once again experience play firsthand rather than vicariously. We need to change people's orientation "from instant replay to instant we-play."[2]

Cooperative community should always be the goal of playing games. After a game is over, players should be better friends than when the game

---

1. Our first game book, *Play It!*, contains even more games than this one! It's still available if you missed it.
2. Matt Weinstein, Joel Goodman, *Playfair* (Impact, 1983), p. 24.

started. Cooperating in a game does not mean that we don't compete; it simply means that we never let competition get in the way of our relationship with everyone else in the game. By making the small effort it requires to change our orientation from competition to cooperation, we can begin to see other players as allies rather than as enemies.

When winning is the goal, the only ones who enjoy the game are those on the winning team and those who feel like they contributed to the win by their great performance. When participating is the goal, both winners and losers have fun because merely playing the game gives them pleasure.

HOW TO CHOOSE THE RIGHT GAME

With over two hundred games in this book, you won't have to worry about finding a game to play. There are more games in this book than you'll ever need. Your problem will be deciding which game is the "right" game to play. That's a good problem to have.

A right game is a game that works for your particular group of players. A wrong game is a game that doesn't work for your group. How do you tell which games will work and which won't? Here are some elements to consider:

1. Safety. Any game is wrong if people are likely to be hurt. Of course, any game can result in an accidental injury; but sometimes people are hurt because reasonable precautions are not taken. When you present a game to others, they assume you have taken every precaution for their safety. Here are some safety suggestions for any game you play:

• Make sure that you have played—or have watched someone else play—any game that you decide to use.

• Take extra precautions when very small children or the elderly are playing with you.

• Do not encourage players to play roughly.

• Check the playing area for protruding objects, hard surfaces, obstacles, slippery floors, or any hazard that might endanger one of the players.

• If you change or adapt a game, think through how those changes affect the safety of the players.

• Athletes enjoy competition and winning. Encourage the more athletic players not to dominate a game by playing too aggressively. If they continue to play too roughly, give them some kind of handicap, such as hopping on one leg or using only their left hands.

• Double check your insurance coverage to make sure all injuries will be covered adequately.

• Always have adequate first aid equipment on hand.

• When you sponsor a large, day-long game event with young people, require parental release forms permitting immediate care to be given to any players who are injured.

NOTE: Make every effort to include the handicapped in your game playing. People too readily assume the handicapped cannot play, when a minor adjustment to the rules would make it possible for them to join the game. Even severely handicapped individuals can be included as referees, official game photographers, or scorekeepers.

2. **Age of group.** Although nearly every game in this book can be played by any person, regardless of age, certain games are more suitable for specific ages. Cooperative games requiring little physical contact work best with a group of families, for instance. On the other hand, high school guys enjoy high-energy games with lots of physical contact.

3. **Sex.** In spite of legitimate concerns about sexism, it's usually best to separate the sexes for physical, hard-hitting games. Although girls may enjoy playing physical games, it's often best if they don't play these games co-ed.

4. **Size of group.** Games like "Ultimate Elimination," for example, don't play well with a small group; games like "Tarzan Kickball," on the other hand, work fine. When you choose a game, consider how it will work with the size of your group.

5. Personality. Every group has a unique personality—its group dynamics. Some groups are active, outgoing, and physical, while others are more easygoing or sophisticated. It's good to give a group new experiences; it's also good to start with a game that the group feels comfortable playing. The secret is not to choose games solely on the basis of whether you enjoy them. Rather, choose games that your group will find enjoyable.

6. Ability. Some actions certain people can't do. For example, little children have a hard time balancing cups of water on their heads; older people have a more difficult time hopping around a football field. Take into account the ability of your group when planning any game.

7. Purpose. Beyond the overall purpose of building community and having fun, games can serve many purposes: wearing out restless campers on the first and last nights of camp; helping people become better acquainted; and providing good healthy exercise.

Remember— games are for people, and no two people experience games in exactly the same way. These guidelines won't insure that every game you play will work perfectly, but they will help.

ADAPTABILITY

Games may be played anywhere, anytime, with anyone. Even so, every group has at least one person who will only play a game by the official rules on an official field with official equipment. While it's true that many games are best played under official conditions, any game may be adapted to fit any set of circumstances. Adaptability simply means that games were meant to be played and that whatever has to be done to get people to play and enjoy themselves should be done.

1. Adapting the rules. Rules tell you how to play a game a certain way. That doesn't mean you can't play the game a different way. If the rules are getting in the way of the game, then change them to make the game better. For example, if your group is playing baseball and no one can hit the ball because the pitching is too fast, make a rule that pitches have to be slow. Remember, playing games is supposed to be fun.

2. **Adapting the time.** As long as people are having fun, time limits are irrelevant. You are free to interrupt or shorten a game if it's boring; you are free to lengthen a game if everyone is enjoying it. Time can be an asset to game playing if you control the time rather than letting it control you.

3. **Adapting the weather.** Well—not really. You can't change the weather, but you can change the game to accommodate the weather. Although you can't keep it from raining on your volleyball game, you can still play volleyball in the rain, play volleyball in raincoats, or play mud volleyball. Bad weather, within reason (you obviously can't play during a tornado or blizzard), should never stop a game.

4. **Adapting the equipment.** Almost every game requires some kind of equipment. You should, of course, always try to get the kind of equipment that will contribute to the best play possible. But you aren't a slave to equipment. If you can't find a volleyball, use a soccer ball, four-square ball, or whatever you can find. If what you find looks like it will affect the outcome of the game, then change the rules. You can play broom hockey with a volleyball, soccer ball, grapefruit (yes, grapefruit), or even two T-shirts wadded up.

HOW TO PLAY A GAME

You can't tell others how to play a game if you haven't played the game or seen it played. If the basic rules and instructions of the game aren't understood by everyone, the result may be mass confusion. That means you must have everyone's attention while explaining the game. Never try to shout directions over the noise of an inattentive group. Get the group's attention by sounding a good referee's whistle (inexpensive whistles are never loud enough) or marine boat horn (keep the boat horn in a secure place because if it's pointed toward a person's ear at close range, it can do some serious damage). It's a good idea to begin a game time with the following permanent rule: Whenever the horn or whistle is sounded, everyone must sit down immediately and be quiet. Use a bullhorn or public address system when instructing large groups.

Enthusiastically explain the basic rules of a game simply, clearly, and as quickly as possible. Make your explanation sound like as much fun as playing the game itself. Demonstrate exactly how the game is to be played. (It's usually easier to show the group how to play than it is to tell them how to play.) Then play a couple practice rounds rather than letting people ask a million "what-if" questions. Most questions are answered while actually playing.

CHOOSING TEAMS

Choosing teams embarrasses those who have the misfortune of being chosen last, especially if they're always chosen last or think they are. If a game requires teams, just before introducing it play a game that automatically puts everyone into groups. These groups can then become teams before anyone realizes what happened. However, since most of the games in *Play It Again!* do not require normal abilities (running with a balloon between your knees?), the quality of the team is not determined by size, strength, or athletic ability. All you need for a good team is a group of people who want to play.

REFEREES

Every game requires several responsible people to help conduct and supervise the games, especially with large groups of players. A good ratio is one leader for every twenty players. When looking for volunteer referees, you'll find there are two types: the Letter-of-the-Law ref and the Fun-and-Games ref. The first type believes referees are authority figures whose main function is to enforce the rules to the letter. Those kinds of referees are fine in the National Football League, but not anywhere else.

The Fun-and-Games ref, on the other hand, understands that rules are nothing more than guidelines to make a game enjoyable and that infractions occur when people's enjoyment of the game is in jeopardy. He believes that rules exist for the benefit of the people playing the game, rather than the people existing for the benefit of the rules. That means that if one team is desperately behind, the referee becomes more observant of the winning team and less observant of the team that is behind.

Clearly identify the referees by asking them to wear striped jerseys, florescent jackets, or bright hats. Make certain that all the referees thoroughly understand the rules of the game. If the referees have to keep referring to the book, they are not familiar enough with the game. Practice the game first with a test group to work out any situations not explained in the rules.

POINTS

Many groups use points to tabulate the standings of teams during game events. As silly as it may sound, the amount of points you give can actually increase the enjoyment and excitement of those who are playing. Points are free, so you don't have to be stingy with them. Give lots of points—a thousand points! Three thousand points! After all, who wants to play a game for fifty measly points when he or she can win three thousand points? Live a little—give ten thousand points!

Now that we have the preliminaries out of the way, you can start doing what you're supposed to be doing—playing. We honestly hope that the games you play from now on will be fun and enjoyable, that they will bring you closer to the people you play with, and that Play It Again! will help you rediscover the joy of game playing.

OUTDOOR GAMES FOR LARGE GROUPS

Blind Flamingo Kickball

Played on a regular baseball diamond, this crazy kickball game requires two teams—one in the field and one at bat (or "at kick"). Use regular kickball rules with the following variations. Fielders must hold one leg up behind them by the hand, "flamingo" style, and must throw wrong-handed (lefties throw right-handed and vice versa). Kickers are blindfolded. Coaches position themselves at each base to yell out directions to their runners. It's as hilarious to watch as it is to play.

Buzzards and Eagles

This is a good game for camps, where you have a large group and play area. Divide players into four teams and give them bird names like "Buzzards," "Eagles," "Turkeys," "Hawks." Then designate a headquarters for each team that is an equal distance from what will be called the "central nest." Also mark off an area designated as "bird hospital," complete with a resident veterinarian. The object of the game is for each team to transport eggs from its own headquarters to the central nest. Each egg is worth 1,000 points.

Give the teams an equal number of eggs—real ones or the plastic, colored Easter eggs. Each team will also need a "portable nest"—that is, a common bathroom plunger! Finally, players need a feather or a strip of cloth to tuck into their waistbands as in flag football. Don't allow kids to tie the strips to their jeans or tuck them in so far that they're hidden.

Once each team has its eggs at its own headquarters, on your signal players may begin transporting eggs to the central nest, but only in the portable nest—no other way. Obviously, several trips back and forth will be required for each team since the portable nest will only hold a few eggs.

Players may try to keep members of other teams from transporting their team's eggs by "plucking" them—that is, by pulling their opponents' flags, flag-football style. Anyone who is plucked must stay with the vet at the bird hospital for five minutes before returning to play.

Players who pluck opponents who are carrying a portable nest filled with eggs may take those eggs to their own headquarters and use them to score points for their own teams. Players may not steal or break another team's portable nest, however. Players are also forbidden to enter their opponents' headquarters. To keep this game from getting too rough, rule out tackling or holding players down in order to pluck them.

Besides the score for eggs, you may award a team additional points each time its members pluck someone. Just have the plucker and the "pluckee" report in.

To vary the game at a camp with a large counseling staff, form only two teams—the counselors are the Buzzards, whose only job is to run around plucking Eagles (the kids) and making them drop their eggs as they run for the central nest.

Duckball

Try this game of kickball—with a twist. The pitcher rolls a playground ball toward the kicker (a one-pitch limit if the group is large), and the kicker kicks away. (To play indoors, use a Nerf ball.) Before running to first base, however, kickers are handed a fully inflated balloon that they must tuck between their knees and keep there as long as they run or are on base. Fielders, meanwhile, are also equipped with balloons between their knees (except the pitcher, who must not assist either team at all) and must waddle as best they can to retrieve the ball and attempt to put the runners out.

Outs are made by touching runners with the ball, either by a tag or a throw. Balls overthrown out-of-bounds limit a runner to a single base, as in baseball.

Points are scored when runners cross home plate with their balloons intact—but that's not the only way. If fielders pop their balloons, the kicking team scores a point. Likewise, if runners pop their balloons, the fielding team scores a point. The game ends when a team earns twenty points or when a predetermined number of innings have been played.

You'll need fifty to sixty balloons in a large plastic bag or trash can to begin the game, and perhaps more as the game progresses. The kids who don't want to play may maintain the balloon supply and hand balloons to runners on their way to first base.

Field Handball

For this football-soccer hybrid, you'll need a large ball (soccer ball, football, volleyball—even a playground ball will do), two durable chairs, and tape, spray paint, or rope to mark off the goal circles. Pylons to mark the field boundaries and arm bands to distinguish teams are optional.

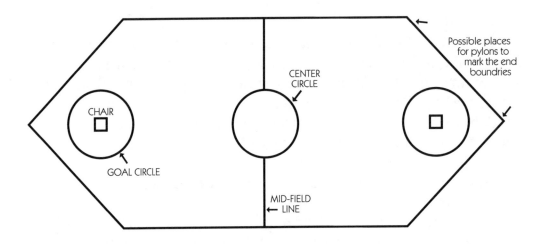

The goal of play is simply to hit with the ball the opponent's chair—which sits empty in the center of a twelve-foot-diameter goal circle at the end of the field. Here's how it's played:

• Players may run with the ball or pass the ball to teammates.

• A ball runner who is tagged has three seconds to pass the ball to a teammate; otherwise, the other team takes possession on the spot. A goal cannot be scored during these three seconds.

• If a player drops a pass from a teammate, any opponent picks up the ball and continues play. An intercepted pass is also played without a break.

• If a defender or attacker enters either of the goal circles, the ball changes possession and play is renewed at the nearest boundary line.

• Following a goal, play begins again in center field as in soccer.

• Using a referee helps curtail unnecessary roughness, which earns the offender a loss-of-possession penalty or temporary removal from the game.

Four Team Crab Soccer

Mark off a square in a field using cones placed about twenty-five yards apart, place a four-foot diameter beach ball in the center, and set up four

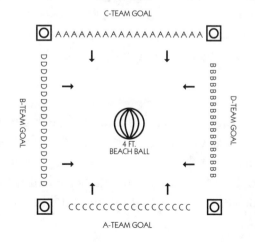

teams of about ten people each as shown on the diagram *(the field can be enlarged or made smaller to accommodate your group size)*.

At the sound of a whistle, players move "crab style" from their team goal to the beach ball in the center. The object of the game is for team members to kick the beach ball across the field of play through the markers of the team opposite them. Because of the size and weight of the beach ball, players are allowed to use their hands to protect themselves from the ball but not to advance the ball.

Frisbee Bull's-Eye

This two-part game works best with thirty kids or more. Form them into three or four teams, then announce the first part: competition in a stated game (it doesn't matter what game) in order to earn frisbees. First place is awarded five Frisbees; second place, three Frisbees; third place, two; and last place, one.

Now for part two. Each team appoints a thrower. Throwers are entrusted with floating their teams' Frisbees onto a horizontal target (three concentric circles on the ground) from behind a line about twenty feet away from the target. Throwers score ten points for their teams if a Frisbee lands within the innermost circle, five points if within the next circle, and one point if within the outer circle.

Teams can play as many rounds as they like, allowing most of a team's players the chance to throw the Frisbees.

Holy Man

The gurus in your group will love this hide-and-seek game, perfect for summer evenings. Select one of your teens to be "Holy Man," who—dressed in an identifying robe or hat—takes a lighted candle and hides somewhere within the boundaries of the game. When Holy Man is settled, the other kids—each armed with a squirt gun and an unlighted candle—

spread out to find him.

When kids discover Holy Man, they light their own candles from his and then, by stealth more than speed, try to get back to a designated home base before their candles are extinguished by others' squirt guns. (Holy Man's candle cannot be extinguished by other players.) Players whose flames get doused must return to Holy Man to relight their candles. The first player to arrive at home base with a lighted candle is the winner.

But if the players' candles get squirted out and they have to return to the Holy Man for a light, they shouldn't expect to find him in the same place—for he can move around at will and hide somewhere new.

Hurl Hockey

With one or two dozen plastic gallon milk jugs, you can play a fast, fun court game that's a mix of hockey and jai alai.

Cut the bottoms out of the jugs in order to make a scoop that can also hurl a ball toward a goal (see diagram). One way to create a goal is to

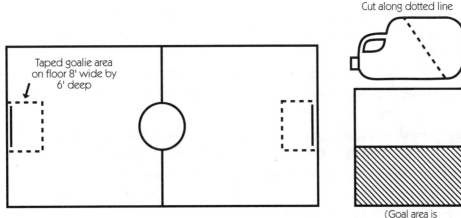

Cut along dotted line

Taped goalie area on floor 8' wide by 6' deep

(Goal area is shaded)

split a ping-pong table in half and set each half at one end of the court; the goal is below the mid-stripe. Use masking tape to mark off an 8' by 6' goalie box in front of each goal.

The game itself is played like hockey, though with a soft, baseball-size ball instead of a puck; the ball can be scooped off the floor with the plastic "gloves" and passed or hurled at the goal. Here are the details:

- Start the game with a hockey-type face-off.
- With the ball in their gloves, players can take only three steps, then must pass the ball or hurl it at the goal.
- The ball can be touched only by the plastic glove, not by feet or by a player's free hand.
- Traveling (taking more than three steps) or out-of-bounds results in the nearest goalie putting the ball back into play.

Inner Tube Baseball

On a softball field, one team fields and the other team "bats" using an inner tube instead of a ball. Batters pick up the inner tube at home plate and rotate seven times, heaving the inner tube into the field on the seventh rotation. As the batter rotates, his or her team may count out loud to help cue the batter when to release the tube. (If you wish, have available several sizes of inner tubes so kids can choose one appropriate to them.) Although there are three bases as in softball, there is no out-of-bounds, so the inner tube may be released in any direction once seven rotations have been completed.

Players are only out when tagged with the inner tube. There are no forced outs or pop flies. Defensive players may tag a base runner by touching the runner with the tube or by throwing the tube at the runner. Any time base runners come in contact with the tube, they are out (unless they are on base, of course).

The only penalty in this game is called "jamming," which occurs when a defensive player tries to "cream" a base runner with the tube (unnecessary roughness). Jamming is a judgment call on the part of the umpire. Award the offended team with a run, and allow the base runner to advance to the closest base. Without this rule, some players will attempt to start another game called maul ball, which is not recommended for most amateur "Inner Tube Baseball" players.

The last rule—the umpire can add or subtract any rules at any time to make the game fun and exciting. All umpire rulings are final.

Kick Golf

No green fees for this round of golf. Set up your own nine-hole course: Hula-Hoops are the greens, small sticks stuck within them are the flags, and small playground balls are the golf balls. Roll the ball up against the stick, and consider it a hole.

For each hole, lay a marker to show where players tee off. And don't forget to set par—use hills and other obstacles or traps to vary the difficulty of each hole. Distribute score cards, and play by teams if you like.

Lightning Strikes

For this game you need a dark night, a large open place like a football field or even an empty parking lot, a few old sheets or blankets, and a glow ball—a ball that glows when you break a cylinder of florescent liquid and put it inside the ball. Divide the group into two teams. Within each team form groups of between three and eight kids and give them a sheet. Align the groups on the field in zones between two goals (as in football) according to the following diagram:

(Arrows show direction of the teams' efforts)

Holding the edges of the sheet and quickly stretching it taut, group members use it to fling the ball toward their goal at the end of the field. Group members get to fling the ball only when it lands in their zone. Each goal earns ten thousand points. Any throwing of the ball by hand, of course, earns ten thousand points for the other team.

The visual effect at night is neat—the eerie glow zips and zigs and zags through the darkness. With enough kids, you may want to use more than one ball.

Missionary

In this game, each team must guide its "missionary" safely through a field of "headhunters" (the opposing team). You'll need to divide the group into two teams of equal size.

The first team to be the missionaries must choose one of its members to travel through a dangerous mission field (see diagram below).

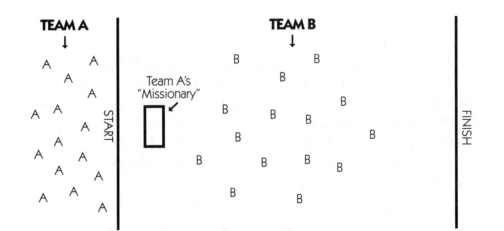

That player must put a paper bag over his or her head and move across the playing field from a starting line to a finish line while trying to avoid being touched by any of the headhunters. Teammates guide the missionary across the field by shouting directions to him or her. Teammates cannot walk with the missionary. (Hint: Teammates must coordinate their directions and shout them in unison to avoid confusing the missionary.)

Meanwhile, the other team plays the part of the headhunters, and spreads out over the playing field at random. The headhunters attempt to impede the progress of the missionary by touching him or her. They may not, however, move from their original positions on the field, except once during each round when they may take three giant steps in any direction. Any contact with the missionary must be made while a headhunter is standing still, so these steps must be planned carefully. The headhunters may also shout false instructions to the missionary, but silence is often a better strategy.

Each team has one chance to guide a missionary and one chance to be headhunters. The missionary is timed from the starting line to the finish line, with a penalty of twenty seconds added for every contact with a headhunter. The team with the lowest time wins.

Nighttime Football

For a wild football game at night, insert one of those glow sticks into the end of a Nerf football. This will enable receivers to see the ball if the lighted end is pointed at them in passing downs. It's a lot of fun.

Nonstop Cricket

I say, how 'bout a game of English "Nonstop Cricket"? Using the diagram to guide you, make a bat (or use a similar wooden paddle), make wickets from old broomsticks and a base block, and buy a foam ball. Form two teams of six to eleven participants—the fielders and the players. Choose a wicket keeper from the fielders and a score keeper from among nonplayers (or have a batter record the runs).

To play (see diagram below):

• The batter attempts to hit the ball with the paddle and on a hit must run to touch the scoring line and return to his crease, so scoring a run.

• Meanwhile, the fielders (the field surrounds the wicket instead of spreading out only in front of the wicket) return the ball to the bowler, who immediately bowls (pitches) to the batter, aiming to hit the wicket, whether or not the batter has returned to the crease.

• The batter must run on the third bowl or forfeit a turn.

• The whole of the batting side is out if a fielder takes a full catch.

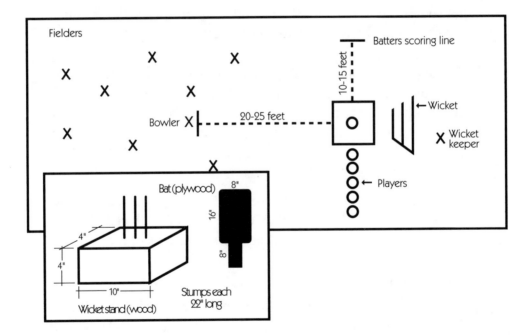

• The batter is out if the wicket is hit by the bowler, a bowl hits the leg of the batter in front of the wicket, the ball is returned by a fielder and hits the wicket before the batter returns to the crease, or the wicket keeper hits the wicket with the ball while the batter is out of the crease.

• The batters keep playing until the last batter is out. The batters then become the fielders, and fielders the batters. Play for a set time or until an agreed score is reached. After a trial run, adjust boundaries or rules. The bowler bowls underhanded.

Parachute Kickball

Mark off a hundred-foot square in the church parking lot or in a field. Divide players into two teams. One team stands within the square, each of its members helping hold a parachute or large sheet. The other team stands outside the square, either scattered around it or together in a line; this team has a soccer or playground ball.

The object for the outside team is to take turns kicking a high, arching kick that lands within the square. If the ball lands within the square—and is not caught by the parachute—then the kicking team gets a point. If the ball is caught by the parachute or if the kicked ball lands outside the square or if the kick is judged to be insufficiently high or arching, then an out is called against the kicking team. Like baseball, teams trade places after three outs.

Pillow Hockey

In this variation of "Broom Hockey" (*Play It!*), the hockey sticks are pillowcases loosely stuffed with crumpled newspapers and tied off. With these "sticks," players hit a playground ball into a goal, hockey fashion.

Lay the available pillows out on the court (an equal number on both sides of the court), then call for teams to select players to run out to the court, grab a pillowcase, and immediately begin playing. When one side scores, call for new players from each team.

What makes this game fun is that it's difficult to hit the ball with much force, or even to hit it at all. Also, unlike Broom Hockey, players don't get smacked accidentally by wooden broom handles.

Puzzle Relay

You'll need five sponsors, a large gymnasium or field, and two new twenty-five-piece children's jigsaw puzzles.

Prepare for the game by doing the following:

• Mark one puzzle box with an X, and mark the back of each piece from that puzzle with an X as well.

• Mark the other box with a Z, and mark each of the corresponding pieces with a Z.

• Mark sixteen small envelopes with an X, place one piece from the X puzzle in each envelope, and seal them. Put the nine remaining pieces back in their box.

• Do likewise for the sixteen pieces from the Z puzzle.

• Set up a big table at home base, then designate five checkpoints about thirty to forty yards away from home.

• Of the thirty-two envelopes, give to each of four sponsors four X envelopes and four Z envelopes.

• To the fifth sponsor give the two puzzle boxes.

• Assign one sponsor to each checkpoint; the sponsor with the boxes goes to checkpoint five.

Now divide the group into an X team and a Z team. Choose a team captain for each team, then divide both teams into four equal subteams. While the two team captains stay at home base, each subteam makes the round of the checkpoints in a different order:

Subteam A: 1-2-3-4-5   Subteam C: 3-4-1-2-5

Subteam B: 4-1-2-3-5   Subteam D: 2-3-4-1-5

The entire subteam must travel to and from each checkpoint together. The sponsor at each checkpoint requires each subteam to perform a task (make up ahead of time a list of tasks appropriate for your own group); upon completion of the task, the sponsor gives the subteam one envelope for its team's puzzle. Here are sample tasks:

Checkpoint 1: Sing one verse of "Pharaoh Pharaoh."

Checkpoint 2: Recite John 3:16 backwards.

Checkpoint 3: Sing "Deep and Wide" with hand motions while running in place.

Checkpoint 4: Form a six-person pyramid and recite the pledge of allegiance.

Checkpoint 5: (captain only) Do an impersonation of Elvis Presley.

Each subteam must return to home base after each checkpoint and hand the envelope to its captain. The captain will put the unopened envelopes on the table. When all the envelopes are in and the entire team—that is, all four subteams—has returned to home base, the team captain must then go to checkpoint five, complete the task given, and return to home base with the box containing the remaining pieces to the team's puzzle. The envelopes are then torn open and the puzzle is completed by the team. The first team to complete its puzzle wins.

Reverse Garbage Bag Soccer

Fill a garbage bag with inflated balloons and twist-tie it. Wrap the bag with masking tape to reinforce the bag, and use it for a soccer ball. Set up the field like regular soccer, but reverse the rules of play as follows: The fielders may not kick the soccer ball, but must use their hands to hit or throw the ball to other players. Fielders incur a penalty for kicking the ball.

The goalie, on the other hand, is not allowed to use his hands—he blocks goals by using his body and feet. Keep an extra garbage-bag soccer ball on hand in case you bust one.

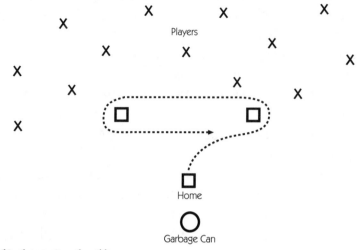

Swedish Baseball

This variation of baseball is most effective with twenty-five or more participants. One team fields while another team of the same size is up to bat. No bats or balls are used, however—all you need is a Frisbee (see diagram on page 32).

The batter comes to the plate and throws the Frisbee out into the field. The fielding team chases down the Frisbee and returns it to a garbage can placed next to home plate. The challenge is that the Frisbee must be tossed in rather than simply dropped in. Meanwhile, the batter runs about ten feet to two bases about eight feet apart with a baseline parallel to home plate. The runner circles the bases, earning for the batting team one point for every lap. The runner continues until the Frisbee is in the can. All the players on the batting team get to be up each inning. There are no outs.

After two or three innings, the score can get quite high. You'll need to have a scorekeeper who can keep track of all the points.

Tarzan Kickball

Some of the old basic games are great to play with a little jazzing up. "Tarzan Kickball" is a perfect example. You'll need the following to play:

- Kickball area—a parking lot or field (a gym will even work, with variations).
- Playground ball (the kind that is low pressure and bouncy).
- Portable sound system—the louder the better.
- A prerecorded cassette of bits and pieces of fast-moving motion picture soundtracks (Rocky movies are great). You can also throw in excerpts of old musicals like *Oklahoma*. Local libraries are excellent resources for this stuff—it's free, too. You'll also need to edit onto the tape at irregular intervals a Tarzan-type yell. Make your cassette about thirty-five minutes long with ten to fifteen Tarzan yells interspersed throughout the recording.
- Two teams.
- Scorekeeper and judge.

The game is played with all the traditional kickball rules. There are two ways to score: scoring regular runs in the kickball game and receiving bonus points for all of the team members getting to their base (bases are wherever you designate them to be) when they hear the Tarzan yell. While the game is going, play the background music to create an exciting atmosphere. Whenever players hear the Tarzan yell, they immediately stop what they are doing and run as quickly as possible to their team's home base. The first team to get all its players squatting down in the team's home base gets ten bonus points. Once the winner is determined for that particular Tarzan yell, play resumes as normal. It takes teamwork. Every player has to be listening carefully and playing at the same time.

All bases are cleared at every Tarzan yell, but runners return to their original positions after the Tarzan break. Rather than use the three-outs system, let each team bat all the way around and then switch. That way everyone has a chance to bat. A judge is needed to see which team gets to its home base first. Orange cones can be used to designate the home bases for each team; make the base small so players have to squish together.

To play longer, just rewind the tape.

The Amoeba That Ate Manhattan

All you need for this game is a clearly defined area (ball field, large room) and lots of kids—though smaller groups will enjoy it, too. Two people are designated the young "amoeba," who immediately join hands and try to capture others by encircling them. Those so captured join the growing chain and continue the quest, running roughly single file until they surround a victim and close the circle.

As each amoeba grows, it may capture groups of people at a time, or even another, smaller amoeba. The game ends when the entire group is part of a single amoeba, and the winner is the last one caught.

Time Warp Tag

Here's another crazy version of the most famous of all games. While playing a regular game of tag, players listen for the blow of a whistle. At the sound, players (including IT) must slow down to a speed equal to a sport replay "slo-mo." In other words, they must do everything in slow motion. Kids will soon get the hang of it and begin to exaggerate their motions.

Make sure the kids do everything in time warp state, even talking and shouting. The game can be played in total time warp, or you can blow the whistle for start/stop intervals. Limit the size of the playing area so that several players have a chance to become IT.

Toilet Tag

This version of tag brings a new flush to that time-tested game. Mark off the playing area suitable for your size group. Designate one or more players to be IT. IT runs around attempting to tag other players, who are then "dead" and must kneel down on one knee with one arm out and to the side. Dead players can reenter the game only when a free player sits on the dead player's knee and pulls down the extended hand—"flushes the toilet." The game ends when all the players except IT are kneeling.

Ultimate Elimination

If you have thirty or more kids and a big playing field, this tag-ball game can continue for a long, exciting time. Players should pair off and tie themselves together at the arm. Throw into the fray several Frisbees or Nerf balls or playground balls—or a combination of them—and it's every pair for itself. When one person of a pair is hit, he or she can no longer throw, but can only defend the partner. When the partner is hit as well, that pair is out of the game altogether—that is, until the pair that finally eliminated them is itself eliminated. When that happens, the first pair can join the game again.

Just when you think the game is winding down, a lethal pair that eliminated several other pairs is itself eliminated—and competition picks up quickly as those renewed pairs begin to play again.

Ultimate Frisbee Football

Here's Ultimate Frisbee with a tackle twist that's guaranteed to tire the most rambunctious junior-high boys. It requires no equipment and lets everyone play quarterback and receiver.

Play on a football-type field with goal lines at either end. The object is to cross the goal line with the Frisbee. As in Ultimate Frisbee, play consists not in running (yet), but in passing the Frisbee in order to move it down field.

Here's the shift to football—if the Frisbee holder does not throw it by the time a covering opponent counts to ten, the Frisbee holder is free to run with the Frisbee—and also free to be tackled by the opposite team if he does not throw on the run to a teammate. The Frisbee changes teams in the case of a tackle, an interception, or an incomplete pass.

Velcro War

For this textile tag game, go to a craft store and purchase golf-ball-size plastic balls and Velcro strips. Use a hot-glue gun to attach the strips to the balls. (The more balls you have, the better the game.)

Then declare a Velcro war among the kids. All combatants must wear a fluffy wool sweater to qualify them to carry "weapons" (the prepared plastic balls). They should also wear some kind of eye protection. In the church or at a school, identify a playing area that includes lots of hiding places accessible by more than one route.

The following rules will get you started. Once it's all-out war, make up the rules as you go along.

• Once a Velcro ball sticks to a player's sweater (players are not allowed to remove balls), that player is wounded. Three wounds equal a kill.

• Play the game as teams, like a lethal version of "Capture the Flag" (*Play It!*). The smaller the group, however, the better it is to play every man for himself.

• The target area can be expanded by requiring all players to wear wool caps.

• The harder players throw the balls, the less likely they are to stick and the more likely they are to injure, so tell the kids to attack with lobs and crafty tosses.

C H A P T E R

3

OUTDOOR GAMES FOR SMALL GROUPS

Crazy Baseball

Create teams of five or more players. With a Nerf ball and bat, play as in regular baseball. Here's the crazy part: After a hit, batters can run to any base—but they may not run through the pitcher's circle. Base runners score, not by touching home plate but by touching all three bases—first, second, and third—though in any order. Teams get six outs.

Croquet Pool

Mark off with rope a 30' by 20' area of smooth ground—this is your "pool table." For pockets lay on their sides speed cones, small buckets, and so on, at the corners and at the midpoint of the thirty-foot sides, pool-table fashion. With enough croquet balls for your group (pool uses sixteen), designate one the cue ball and begin the game by breaking the "triangle," using the croquet mallet.

From here the game is played just like pool: the first team (or player) to "sink" its croquet balls into the cones wins. Mark the balls by color, stripe, and so on. And don't forget to save the eight ball for last!

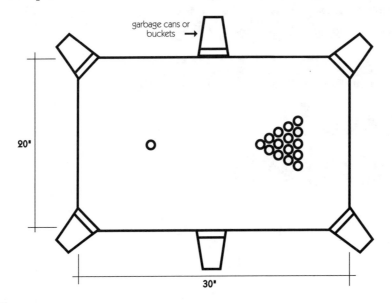

garbage cans or buckets →

20"

30"

Frisbee Swat

What you'll need for this indoor/outdoor active game are two (or more) Frisbees, two chairs, two cones (or two-liter soda bottles), two teams, and a pillow polo stick or rolled-up newspaper for each player. At each end of the playing area, place a chair with a cone on its seat. The goal of each team is to knock the other team's cone off the chair with a Frisbee. Points are awarded for each knock down.

Team members pass the Frisbees to each other as they work their way down the field. No one is allowed to run with the Frisbee—they can only pass it. Team members hold a pillow polo stick or newspaper in one

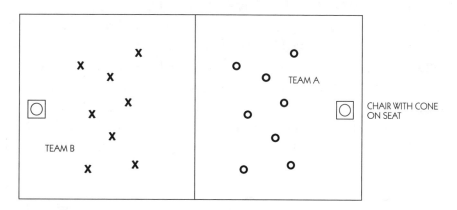

hand, which is used for knocking down the opponent's Frisbee, and they use their other hand to catch and throw their team's Frisbee. To play the game, teams must attempt to score on offense and at the same time maneuver around on defense to swat the opponent's Frisbee out of the air.

Human Pinball

Give a playground ball to a group of at least ten, then explain the following rules:

• The object is to be the last one standing. Players who are hit with the ball and fail to catch it must kneel. If a player catches a thrown ball, the thrower must kneel.

• When players get the ball, in order to throw it, they cannot run or walk with it—they must throw from where they obtained the ball.

• Though they cannot move around, kneelers can still play while on their knees. They can stand again if they touch a standing person or hit someone with the ball. Those who are touched or hit must kneel.

This game can be played both indoors or outdoors.

Inland Surfing

Who needs a beach for a beach party? Your kids can surf your backyard turf with this board, made from an old ironing board reinforced with 2 x 4 crossbars that are grooved in order for the board to sit on ropes slung between trees (see diagram below). Decorate the top of the "surfboard" with contact paper and automotive striping, supply a mattress or other cushioning for the inevitable wipeouts, then—cowabunga! Surf's up as two people shake the ropes to create "waves" and surfers try their best to ride them out. Run a timed competition—record contestants' best times or the average of several tries.

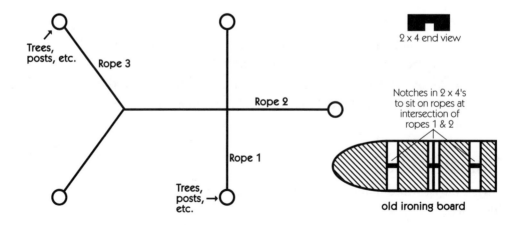

Trees, posts, etc.

Rope 3

Rope 2

Rope 1

Trees, posts, etc.

2 x 4 end view

Notches in 2 x 4's to sit on ropes at intersection of ropes 1 & 2

old ironing board

Inner-Tube Open

This equalizer can be won by sheer inexperience—so look out, golf pros! You'll need one or two nine-iron golf clubs; a dozen tennis balls (six yellow, six orange); a large blanket, quilt, or tarp; and a large, inflated inner tube.

Mark a line ten to twelve feet away from the front edge of the blanket; players take their strokes from behind this line. Place the inner tube on the far edge of the blanket . Players get six strokes to earn points the following ways:

• Ball hits blanket	1 point
• Ball stays on blanket	3 points
• Ball hits inner tube	5 points
• Ball stays inside inner tube	20 points

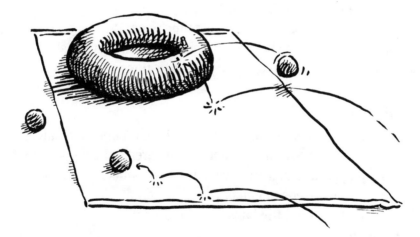

Here's what makes this game fun: points are awarded cumulatively. That is, if a ball hits the inner tube (five points), rolls across the blanket a ways (one point), and remains on the blanket (three points), the player earns nine points. Or if a ball hits the inner tube but bounces away without touching the blanket, that player earns five points. Most points wins. Play by teams or individually.

Pie Tin Toss

For this game you will need to secure the use of six high hurdles, like those used at a track meet. If you can't get real ones, improvise. Line the hurdles up as in a regular hurdle race.

Team members run carrying a pie tin filled with shaving cream. When they come to the hurdle, they must throw the pie tin up, go under the hurdle, catch the pie tin on the other side, and continue until they have gone under all six hurdles. In relay fashion players then run back (no "hurdling" this time) and pass the tins to the next team members in line, who run the course in the same way.

Each team is timed, and the best time wins. Runners who drop a pie tin must go back to the beginning and try again. Replenish the shaving cream in the tins for players dropping their tins at the hurdles.

Pop-Can Bowl

Divide your group into two teams, position them on opposite halves of a recreation room, gymnasium, or other playing area, and supply players with several playground balls. Between the two teams is a three-foot wide "can zone," where dozens of empty pop cans stand.

Players must bowl the balls into the cans in order to knock them into the other team's playing area, without crossing into the can zone themselves. The team with the least cans in its area after two minutes of playing wins.

Power Croquet

For this croquet variation, the bigger and more rugged the yard (or lot or field) the better. Unlike its traditional, genteel cousin, "Power Croquet" is set up with as many obstacles as you can find—or fabricate. For example, set wickets—

- On the bank of a ditch.
- Underneath a parked car.
- So that players must bank their balls off a cement block or a wall to score a wicket.
- So that players must navigate fallen branches.

In short, design a course similar in shape to normal croquet, but one full of obstacles to get over, around, or through. Put the ends of the course as far from each other as possible; if you're confined to a suburban lot, at least run the course around the house through both the front and back yards.

Ring Toss

Played just like the traditional carnival game—except that students are the "bottles" (perhaps with traffic cones on their heads) and Hula-Hoops are the rings. Arrange the game to fit your group or your event; have teams of two take turns tossing the hoops over each other, after each toss taking a step backward to increase the distance between them. Or have students step up to a line one at a time and face a group of bottles, and give each thrower three tries to ring a peer. (The bottles further away from the throwing line are worth more points.)

Score Ball

This variation of baseball is a great equalizer of talent—nonathletic types do as well as your group's jocks. All you need is an indoor or outdoor playing area marked into zones per the diagram below, a bat, and three differently colored Nerf balls.

Divide into two teams. The fielding team spreads out in the "field" while the team at bat sends its first member to the plate to hit. Now here's how "Score Ball" is played:

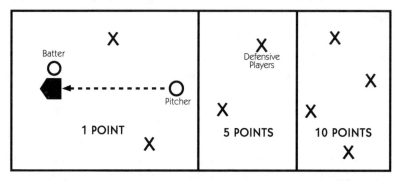

• A batter gets only three pitches; three strikes put him out, as does a fly ball that a fielder catches.

• The three colored balls are pitched in the same sequence for each batter. Here's why: the first pitch (the red ball) is worth one point if it's hit; the second (yellow), two points; the third (blue), three points. Colored balls makes it easy to keep track of the points. So a batter may choose either to hit whatever ball comes his way or to wait for the second or third pitch for more points.

• There's more—the point value of a hit ball is multiplied by the point value of the zone it lands in. For example, if Shelly hits the second pitch (two points) into the middle zone (five points), she earns ten points for her team. A hit, therefore, can earn anywhere from one to thirty points.

Play as many innings as you like!

Tennis Ball Golf

Here's a spin-off from the game "Frisbee Golf" (*Play It!*). Set up a golf course using boxes (big ones for amateurs, small ones for "pros") in a park or some other large open area. Golfers toss a tennis ball, attempting to get it inside the box for each hole. Boxes should be numbered one through nine (or eighteen).

You can make this game as easy or as difficult as you want, depending on the location of the boxes and how the ball is tossed. You can require that all tosses be underhand, through the legs, over the shoulder, bounced, or however you wish. Usually a player will put the ball into the box only to watch it bounce out.

Trac-Ball Tourney

The next two games—an outdoor field game and an indoor gym game—use Trac Ball scoops something like the Mexican jai alai scoops. You can pick up a Wham-O Trac Ball set (two scoops and a ball or two) from most department, toy, or sporting-goods stores.

• **Trac Football.** Remember the variation of football called speedball or razzle dazzle touch football—where the quarterback must pass, and then receivers themselves can pass anywhere on the field in order to move the ball toward the goal? Now play with a Trac Ball set, and you've got "Trac Football."

Only three rules:

1. Play is dead not when the ball carrier is touched or tackled, but when the ball touches the ground. Defensive strategy, then, calls for interfering with a throw or a reception and trying to knock the ball from a carrier's scoop. A team gets four downs in which to score (see rule three about first downs).

2. The ball is advanced only by throwing it using the scoop, not by running it. Players carrying the ball may scramble behind the line of scrimmage (the point at which the play begins or the point at which the ball is caught), but they may not run beyond the line of scrimmage until they hurl the ball. Teammates (potential receivers) may run anywhere, of course.

3. Two complete passes earn a first down. Those passes may come within a play; or one may occur in the first down, the other during the third down. Any time during the four downs that a team completes its second pass, it earns a first down. (If your group gets good at Trac Football, increase the difficulty of earning first downs: require three completes for a first, award two consecutive first downs if a team completes three passes within a single play, and so on.)

Interceptions, kickoffs, hikes, punts—they're all done similarly to regular touch football, but within the limitations imposed by these three rules. Six scoops may be minimum to start out with. Some "Trac Football" players don't think a maximum exists. "The more rackets, the better!" they say.

• **Macho Trac Ball.** This lacrosse-like game will become a favorite of the rough-and-tough guys in your group. Situate two equal teams of any size on opposite sides of a center line. Now supply indoor hockey nets at either end (or draw or tape an area on the two opposite baseline walls, or simply use the closed gym doors as goals if they are at proper ends of the gym).

Equip players with two balls and at least six Trac Ball scoops. The object of the contest is to hurl a ball into the goal defended by the opponents—but at no time can players cross the center line into their opponents' territory. A team may defend its goal by putting as many of its players as it wants in front of the goal. In so doing, they'll get stung a bit by balls flung at their goal, but they'll also be thwarting attempts on their goal by the opposition across the center line.

The twist to this dodging game is the spin that Trac Ball scoops put on the ball. It's hard to judge curves coming at you sixty to eighty miles per hour.

Two-on-Two Basketball

Here's a twist to the standard two-on-two game that's especially adaptable to tournament play. Each two-person team designates one of its members as the stationary shooter—stationary shooters must remain at one end of the free-throw line, they cannot move their feet, and only they can do the shooting for their teams. The remaining person on each team is the moving player. Moving players grab the ball, rebound, block shots, intercept passes—everything but shoot.

Variations are endless. In coed games designate the girls as shooters, the guys as moving players. Or place your shooters anywhere on the court in order to vary the difficulty of the shots. Or add players and designate more shooters or more moving players.

Volley Bounce Ball

This game is great for younger kids as well as challenging to athletes. Lower the volleyball net until the bottom edge touches the floor—or play on a tennis court. Use a bouncy playground ball. The game is like traditional volleyball—six-man rotating teams, volleyball scoring, no more than three hits per team per volley, no two consecutive hits by any one player.

Here are the differences: servers serve as in two-square—they bounce the ball once, then hit it over the net. Teammates can help a lagging serve over the net. The ball may bounce once (but doesn't have to) before the receiving team returns it. The ball may also bounce between the two or three hits a team makes before returning the ball over the net.

INDOOR GAMES FOR LARGE GROUPS

Anatomy Clumps

In this combination of "Anatomy Shuffle" and "Clumps" (both from *Play It!*), players begin by milling around the room as the leader stands in the middle. After a few seconds the leader blows a whistle and yells out two things—a part of the body and a number ("Elbow! Three!"). All players then rush to get into groups of whatever number was called and connect with each other whatever body part was called. After the call "Elbow! Three!," for example, players form groups of three and touch elbows with each other. The last group to correctly do this or a group of players not in a proper group is eliminated from the game.

Other examples: knee (4), nose (3), ankle (6), back (2), rear (5), neck (2), shoulder (6), head (4), lip (2).

Arena Nerfketball

If you have a large room and can mount Nerf ball baskets and backboards at either end (or construct simple, portable frames to mount the baskets), your group can generate all the enthusiasm of a tournament play-off. Divide the group into two teams, who devise team names and cheers. Subgroups of five players rotate in and out every few minutes to give everyone a chance to play. Use refs to maintain order and keep the game moving. Since the baskets may be fragile, tape off the area four feet out from each basket and declare it out-of-bounds.

Other rules that keep the game active—

- Since Nerf balls can't be dribbled, players must pass after taking three steps.
- No touching opponents.
- No roughness.
- Play stops at ref's whistle, and ball goes to ref. (Violation of this rule results in a penalty.)
- All penalties result in a free throw. (Free-throw shooters must rotate.)

• Ref's decisions are final.

A fitting and frenetic finale? Invite everyone onto the floor for the game's last minute!

Bail-O-Wack

Played like volleyball, this game uses a balloon and no net. To set up, use masking tape to make a straight line across the middle of the playing area. The length of the line in feet should be twice the total number of players on both teams. For example, for ten players make a twenty-foot line.

```
TEAM A  X    X    X   (X)   X    X    X
TEAM B  O    O    O   (O)   O    O    O
                       ↑
                   TEAM CENTER
```

Divide the group into two teams that stand in a single row facing each other across the taped line (as if it were the net). Players should stand four feet apart from teammates and two feet back from the line. Players may not move from their starting positions during play, though one foot may leave the floor to kick the balloon if the other stays in place.

The object is for players to volley a balloon back and forth across the line without allowing it to touch the floor on their team's side. The balloon can be batted with hands or kicked. As in volleyball, contact with the balloon alternates between players on the same team, but the balloon cannot be touched by the same player twice in a row. Unlike volleyball, however, teams are not limited to three contacts in order to get the balloon back over the line to their opponents.

The middle player in each team's line is the "center." Each round begins with one of the centers serving by tapping the balloon across the line to the opposing team. The team that won the point in the previous round gets to serve. A team scores a point when the balloon touches the floor on the opposing team's side of the line.

There is no out-of-bounds play, so if a team bats the balloon over the heads of players and out of their reach, the opposing team scores a point. A team also scores a point when a player on the opposing team makes contact with the balloon twice in a row or moves out of position.

You'll need extra balloons in case one bursts, and a referee to make sure players stay in position.

Balloon Bomb

Remember the leftover party balloon that you'd bounce around in the air when you were a child, trying to keep it from hitting the ground? What was rainy day entertainment then still works with youth groups today.

Formalize the game a bit—form two teams that try to hit the balloon away from the opposition, require that teams alternate hits (only one hit per team), and forbid hitting the balloon directly at the floor. Scoring can run like this: intentional grounding scores a point for the opposition, as does two consecutive hits by members of the same team. If the balloon touches the ground, the point goes to the team that hit it last.

Or a variation: Instead of the two teams intermingling in the playing area, put them on opposite sides of a six-foot-wide "dead zone" and permit—volleyball fashion—two hits per team (by different players) before returning the balloon across the dead zone. More than two hits per team or more than one hit per person scores a point for the opposition. If the balloon lands in the dead zone, the point is scored against the team that last hit it. A team serves until it loses a point.

Balloon Bump

Here's an indoor game for moderately sized groups (twenty or more kids). Divide players into groups of four to six or so; place randomly around the room about as many chairs as there are groups; place lots of deflated balloons on each chair; then instruct each group to form a huddle, arms around shoulders, in the middle of the room.

On "go" each huddle shuffles to a chair and one member of the team grabs a balloon and blows it up, ties it off, and drops it into the middle of the huddle of people—who, as they move toward another chair to repeat the process, must keep the balloon off the floor by pressing it

with their stomachs. At the second chair, they must blow up two balloons; at the third chair, three balloons, and so on, all the while maintaining their huddle and keeping their balloons from falling to the floor.

If a balloon falls, the huddle must stop and put it back in their middle again (which takes time). A huddle cannot visit a chair where there is already another huddle working. Call time at three minutes, count how many balloons each huddle has in its middle, announce a winner—and play again!

Banana Rugby

In a large room that's easy to clean, two teams each try to advance a banana over an opposite goal line. The banana can be advanced only by passing it; players may take only two or three steps before throwing the banana. A team loses possession of the banana if a member takes more than the acceptable number of steps before throwing or if a throw becomes an incomplete pass.

Have plenty of bananas on hand; they're reduced to mush quickly. And spiking the banana after a score is not recommended.

Basketcase

Here are the crazy twists to this basketball variation: the ball is carried overhead instead of dribbled down the court and is passed to a teammate by rolling it. Baskets are scored by throwing the ball up through the bottom of the hoop.

Here are some details players need to know:

• Teammates of one who passes the ball may use their hands to pick it up and carry it downcourt.

• Opponents of a passer, however, cannot use their hands to intercept a passed (rolled) ball—they must snare the ball between their feet, after which they can use their hands to carry and pass the ball.

• Foul shots are taken this way: the shooter rolls the ball to a teammate along the key, who may pick it up and make a basket à la "Basketcase."

• Play to twenty-one—the odd point must come from a foul shot.

Basket-Dodgeball

For this game you need a gym or a full basketball court with two hoops, four basketballs, and a playground ball.

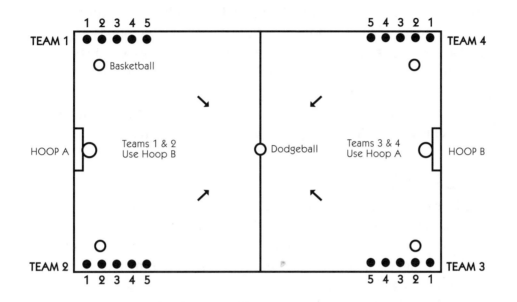

Divide players into four even teams. Each team lines up in a corner of the court in tallest-to-shortest order. Each player on the team is assigned a number—one for the tallest, two for the next tallest, and so on. (To accommodate uneven teams, assign some players two numbers.)

Now to play. After you make sure all players are sitting, yell out a number—"Three!" The four 3s leap up, grab their basketballs, and dribble them to the basket at the opposite end of the gym from them. Only when players make a basket can they run back to their team without dribbling and set down the ball. And here's where dodgeball enters. The first player back from replacing his or her basketball runs to center court, picks up the dodgeball, and begins the dodgeball game. Whichever of the three other active players he hits is out (the ball must hit the person without first bouncing)—unless its intended victim catches the ball, in which case the thrower is out. Woe to the player who's still struggling with making a basket when the other three start dodgeball!

When three players are eliminated from a dodgeball game, the survivor's team earns one point. Return balls and players to starting positions again, then call another number. Play as many rounds as you like, or play until a team reaches a predetermined score. With kids dribbling in opposite directions and two of them shooting at the same basket you'll get some wild collisions.

With few people or only one hoop, form just three teams that shoot in the same basket. Adapt the game for indoors with a Nerf ball.

Boundary Ball

Kids love dodgeball, but as the "kids" become young adults a game of dodgeball can become deadly. Thus, "Boundary Ball."

Divide the group into two teams. If your group combines junior and senior highers, make the competition fair by including kids of both age groups on both teams.

For a playing field, choose an area with a square boundary. A gym, parking lot, or roped-off field all work well. Establish a center dividing line and have teams take their sides.

The game is played by rolling or bouncing the play ball through the opposing team and across the boundary behind the opposing team. The ball must be rolled or bounced. (This eliminates potential bodily injury inflicted by strong-armed throwers.)

Score for Team B if ball crosses this line →   TEAM A HERE   TEAM B HERE   ← Score for Team A if ball crosses this line

The game can be played to twenty-five points (or whatever), one point for each ball that crosses the opponents' back boundary. A referee is helpful, and point judges can be a great help as well in determining whether a point is valid. Points are not valid unless the ball is rolled or bounced over the line.

Double Shuffle Toss

For this fast-moving game, arrange chairs in a circle so everyone has a chair. Add two extra chairs to the circle. Everyone sits in a chair except for the one who's IT—he or she stands in the middle. The sitters keep moving around from chair to chair to prevent IT from sitting down. If IT manages to sit down in a chair, the person on his or her right becomes IT, and the game continues.

But that's not all. As everyone's shuffling from chair to chair, they also pass or throw a rolled towel to anyone in the circle. If IT in the middle intercepts the towel, he or she trades places with the one who threw it. They also trade places if IT can tag the one holding the towel.

For an extra large group, add more people in the middle, more towels, and more empty chairs.

Fuzzyball

Here's a takeoff on baseball perfect for indoors and for groups of ten to fifty. You'll need a "fuzzyball"—one of those softball-sized nursery toys with a rubber center and fabric (usually yarn) covering—and a plastic Wiffle ball bat. (In a pinch you can use a Nerf ball and a broom.) Lay out home plate and three bases, divide players into two teams, and play ball—well, play "Fuzzyball." Here are the differences:

• With a hit, players run first to what is normally third base, then to what is normally first base, then to what is normally second base, then home.

• Runners are put out only by a tag or by being hit below the shoulders by a thrown ball. Catching fly balls and tagging bases are not outs.

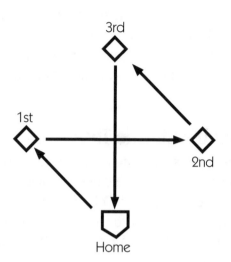

• Everyone on a team gets to bat once, and only once, each inning, regardless of how many outs. (Outs retire runners from base running; they don't determine the length of the inning.)

• The team at bat supplies its own pitcher; a maximum of three pitches are allowed to each batter; two strikes constitute an out.

Group Juggle

This circle game is something like hot potato, with a dash of *Concentration*. Throw a ball to one person in a standing circle of kids. That person throws it to another, and so on until everyone has received and thrown the ball once—but exactly once. No one should get the ball a second time, which means each player needs to remember where the ball's been. If your group's frustration threshold is high, increase the speed of the game and add more balls.

Head Hacky Sack

To each seven-to-ten-person team, give a punch-ball-type-balloon. The teams form circles and try to keep the punch ball in the air using only their heads. Play by the same rules as hacky sack, except that the head is the only part of the body with which players can legally hit the ball. If the punch ball falls to the floor, pick it up and start over. The team with the most consecutive hits is the winner.

Indoor Murderball

Here's an indoor game for two teams. You need at least five on a team, but you can play with a lot more, depending on the size of the room you have. You need a room that is nearly indestructible, with space to run.

Two teams of equal size line up on opposite walls, about three feet from the wall. Team members then number off. A ball is placed in the middle of the room. (Any large ball will work.) The leader calls out a number, and the two players with that number (one from each team) run out to the middle and try to hit the opposite team's wall with the ball. The team standing in front of the wall tries to prevent that from happening.

Players attempt to get the ball to its goal any way they can—carrying it across, throwing, kicking, rolling, whatever. Anything is legal.

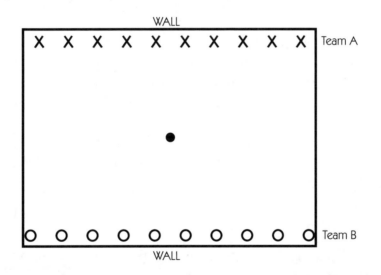

Indoor Soccer

With a large, unfurnished room and a small (six-inch) soccer ball, you can stage your own indoor soccer tournaments. Adjust the rules to suit your own situation and to keep the game swift and safe. Divide larger groups into teams of five—two teams play for two minutes, then are replaced by

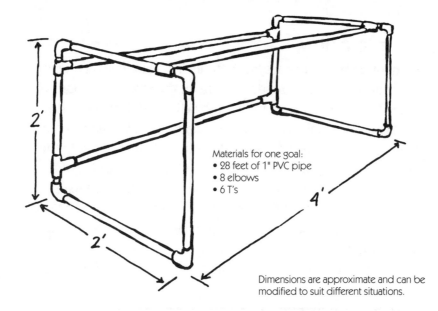

Materials for one goal:
- 28 feet of 1" PVC pipe
- 8 elbows
- 6 T's

Dimensions are approximate and can be modified to suit different situations.

two new teams. Or keep 'em guessing with a tag-team variation—divide a big group into two teams, which divide themselves again into groups of five. At the whistle (blown at varying intervals) players stop playing where they are, run to their sideline, and tag a new group of teammates who can then resume play.

You can construct your own goals with just a few lengths of PVC pipe and some inexpensive cargo netting. So you can disassemble them easily for storage, don't glue the pipe.

Nine-Legged Race

Just for fun or to demonstrate the value of working together, this variation of the three-legged race needs lots of space.

Divide the kids into groups of eight (or so—the numbers don't matter as long as the teams are even.) Place five kids on one side of the playing field, and place the team's remaining three kids opposite the five and across the field. Two players from the five-kid side begin a traditional three-legged race. When they reach the other side, they add another team member, turn, and run back. At each end of their course they tie up with another teammate until all eight kids are strung together at the ankles and running the last length. The first across the finish line wins. (The real fun is watching them figure out how to turn around—but don't tell them this.)

For heightened hilarity, use thin plastic trash bag strips as ties, and add this rule—if a tie breaks, they have to stop and either retie it or replace it.

And even though you may not have specified the game as a foot race, the teammates cannot drop to their knees and pull themselves along with their hands.

Off the Wall

To play this high-energy competition, create a playing court in your gym by assigning each wall a color and taping fifty inflated balloons of that color to the wall. Create a territory for each color that extends twenty feet from the wall, leaving a large "free zone" in the center of the gym. Set a large box to be the "safe" in the center of each territory and mark off an area to be the team's "jail" at the edge of each territory.

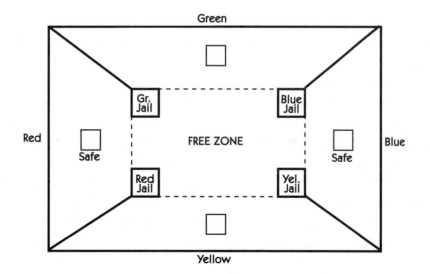

Divide your group into four teams—one for each wall. Each team assigns players to be "defenders" and "invaders," with one person assigned to be the jailer.

Invaders try to hit opposing teams' balloons off the wall with balls (soccer balls or playground balls) thrown from the free zone. Defenders may not return to the wall balloons that are hit off the wall. Invaders may also steal balloons from the wall by invading an opposing team's territory. Stolen balloons are taken back to the invader's own team safe. Invaders may not steal balloons from another team's safe!

Defenders may defend their wall by catching or deflecting balls. They may also capture invaders by tagging them within the territory. Captured invaders are taken to the jail.

A team may "buy out" its invaders who are in jail by exchanging three balloons from its safe for its incarcerated invader. The team holding the invader in jail may then return these balloons to its wall.

At the end of the game, each team earns five points for every balloon on its wall and ten points for every opposing team's balloon in its own team's safe.

Parliff

Make two teams of eight or more kids. Assign one team to spread out near the far wall of a gym while the other team goes up to "bat" at the opposite end of the gym using a basketball. The batter takes the ball and either punts or throws it in any direction (no boundaries). The batter then runs to the far wall, touches it, and runs back to touch the "home" wall. Meanwhile, the team in the "field" is chasing down the ball and passing it to a designated shooter under the basket next to their own home wall.

If the shooter can make the basket before the batter touches his or her own home wall, the batter is out. If the batter makes it home first, her or his team wins a point for the "run." After three outs the opposing team is up. Highest score after nine innings wins.

People Ball

Here's a basketball game that includes everyone, not just the competitive hoopsters. After you divide your group into two teams, five from each team play regulation basketball on the court—except that they cannot dribble the ball. In fact, they cannot move when they have the ball. The remaining team members spread out along both sidelines, alternating players from opposing teams.

Here's how the ball is moved down the floor: The ten players on the court must throw the ball to a sidelines teammate not on the court, who then throws it to a court player on her or his team. There are plenty of chances for interception, of course, both on the sidelines and the court.

Players should wear identifying colors or jerseys for quick recognition. There are no fouls on sideliners, and the ball is always put into play by a sideliner.

Ring-Net Ball

On a basketball court the defense team scatters to cover the "field." From the sideline at mid-court, an offensive team "batter" throws a basketball into the field. The batter then races to the circle at mid-court—the "base"—and runs around it as many times as possible before the defense can grab the ball and sink a basket. Score one point for each completed circle around the base. Everyone on the team throws before the inning switches.

Skizbomania

Using squirt guns as weapons in this search-and-destroy game in the dark, players attempt to hit the targets—pages or pieces of pages from paint-with-water coloring books attached to players' backs. When the lights go on, the winning team is the one with the fewest hits.

You can make the game as elaborate or as simple as you want

with the following modifications:

- To give some indication of the players locations in the pitch-dark room, tag each kid with a strip of glow-in-the-dark tape on a headband or pinned to the shirt front or back. Or use a strobe light.

- If you want players to be able to identify teams in the dark, arrange a few small glow-strips in a team pattern.

- For more accurate scoring, cut the coloring-book pages into quarter-sized circles; then glue, tape, or staple them onto a paper towel, which is pinned to the back or front of a player.

To keep the action going longer, provide a convenient water source to refill the squirt guns.

Switcher

Form six teams of four or more to sit in chairs set up in a hexagon, one chair per team member. Assign each team a number (1 through 6), and give the captain of each team a sign marked with the team number. Players should be seated as teams, in numeric order, clockwise. The object of the game is for each team to switch places with another team when you call a switch pattern.

For instance, calling out the number pattern 1-3, 2-6, 5-4 means that when you yell "Switch!" teams 1 and 3 must exchange places, teams 2 and 6 must exchange places, and teams 5 and 4 must exchange places. (You should list lots of number patterns ahead of time and simply read them off during the game.) Each captain holds high the team sign to help players find their team's new location, but it's still mayhem.

Here's the competitive angle: The last person seated is out (the chair, however, is left in). If the captain goes out, she or he gives the team-number sign to a teammate. Then you call out the next number pattern—"4-2, 1-5, 3-6—Switch!"—and so on, until only one player is left or until there is only one remaining player representing each team. Then let them play the final few rounds. (see diagram next page)

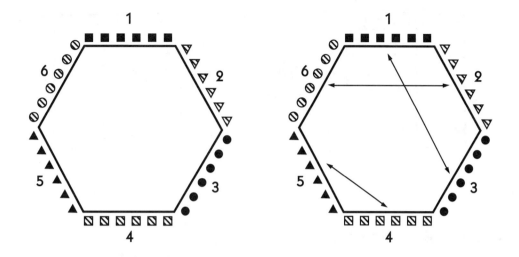

Tapeworms

Set up a table at each end of the playing area, form a semicircular safety zone in front of each table with pylons or chairs, and stick a bunch of two-inch-long pieces of masking tape to the front edge of each table (two pieces per team member).

The game starts as all players pile into their own safety zones, grab one piece of tape each, and then enter the battle zone in order to stick the tape on their opponents' bodies, below the shoulders. Players can't remove the tape once they're stuck. After sticking someone, players can return to their safety zone (for only ten seconds) to get one more piece of tape.

After a specified period of time, the game ends. The team that received the fewest hits wins. Colored tape brightens up the game and can also designate teams. (see diagram on next page)

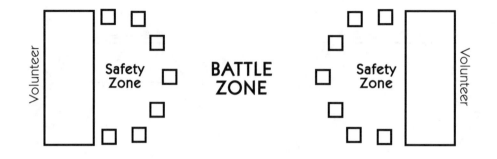

Teddy Bear Football

Although this game sounds corny, bear with us—a little hype and the right mix of humor makes this flag-football perversion more than bearable. In fact, it's actually become an annual event at one church, drawing players and spectators alike.

It's traditional flag football, though played in a gym or fellowship hall—and with a teddy bear instead of a football.

In a gym roomy enough for running, passing, and—yes—kicking a teddy bear, erect goal posts from two-by-fours, or use crepe paper taped to the walls for field-goal markers. In a short gym, for instance, allow only five downs. The ball is given to the other team even if the team in possession makes their yardage for another down. If the team does not score within five downs, it must punt the bear to the other team or try for a field goal on the fifth down. (Be sure to use traditional punting and kicking formations.) You may want to include a girls-only quarter, followed by a boys-only quarter. During the remaining quarters, keep the girls active by requiring that a girl touch the ball once during each possession. In coed teams, of course, limit the physical contact involved in blocking or running over people.

A fifteen-inch bear is just the right size; it will work well for kickoffs, passes, punts, and field goals. (The smaller stuffed bears just don't provide the same level of sadistic pleasure.) KIPP in Indianapolis sells reasonably priced carnival bears (800/428-1153 or 317/634-5507). You may be able to borrow a bear, but the likelihood of returning it the way you received it is slim. In fact, you'll probably need a replacement bear to finish off the game—so get two.

Cue the referee to use creative calls like "Roughing the teddy!" Then play traditional flag football, modifying the rules to fit your situation.

Halftime? Offer a refreshment stand (free snacks), a kazoo marching band, and the crowning of a queen (a guy dressed up like a girl).

Triangle Tag

Have the group divide into teams of four. Three of the group form a triangle, linking hands, with the fourth person in the middle (see diagram). Then, play a regular game of tag. One team is IT and the other teams try to avoid being tagged. The only players who can do the tagging, or be tagged, are the players in the middle of the triangles. As the players in the middle of the

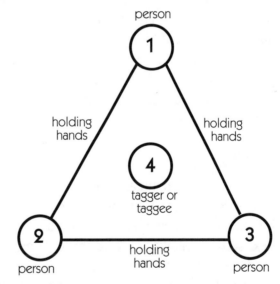

triangles run, the triangles must stay with them at all times, without letting go of their hands. A tag is illegal if the tagging player's triangle is broken.

Turns and Trades

Form two concentric circles of equal numbers of kids facing each other. Tell the kids to trade one thing they have on for one thing the person facing them has on—jewelry, shoes, socks, belts, hats. The players must then put on the items they traded for.

Now ask the inner circle to move three people to their right so that each player has a new partner. Partners must make another trade; but they can not trade anything they've received in a trade. Next ask the outer circle to move two people to their right and repeat the trading process. Call for one more turn and trade.

Kids now have run out of jewelry, shoes, etc, and may be getting embarrassed about another impending trade. So have some fun with them: tell the outer circle to move two people to the right again. You'll hear moans, but when they move, tell them to trade something that has already been traded. Repeat this twice.

Now tell them they have two minutes to retrieve all of their items. Offer a prize to the first one to bring all of the items up to you, or you can time the group to see how quickly they can all retrieve their things and then sit down.

The Wave

"The Wave" is a popular cheer seen at sports events in large stadiums across the country. Usually one section of the stadium begins the Wave by jumping up, throwing hands up in the air, and letting out a cheer. The next section follows suit, and this continues all around the stadium in a kind of domino effect. It really looks like a wave. (Trivia buffs will be interested to know that the Wave is said to have originated at the University of Washington.)

"The Wave" can also be done on a much smaller scale. If you have an auditorium full of people, divide the group into two sections, and try it by rows. The first row in each section begins by standing up, throwing hands up in the air, and letting out a cheer. The second row follows, then the third, and so on to the last row. After the Wave reaches the last row, it can move in reverse back up to the front again. See which side can complete the Wave first.

With even smaller groups, have the kids do the Wave one person at a time. Set it up to go down rows of chairs or around a circle. It really looks crazy when done around banquet tables.

Ultimate Death Ball

Set up a playing field according to the diagram (the size of the field depends on the facilities and number of players). Split the group into two equal teams and give each team a playground ball.

The teams face-off in the main part of the court (A1 and B1 on the diagram) and start throwing the balls at each other. Players hit by a ball thrown from the opposing team's main court must retreat to their own secondary court (A2 or B2 on the diagram). Players who throw a ball that is then caught by an opposing team member must also retreat to the secondary court.

The players stuck in the secondary courts retrieve the balls that get past the players in the main court. They can return to main-court play by

B2	A1	B1	A2

hitting one of the opposing main-court team players with the ball. The hit player in this case, however, remains in his own main court. Only a hit by a main-court player sends players to the secondary court.

This game really works best indoors where the walls and ceiling provide boundaries.

Wall Hockey

Groups of six to fifty kids can play this steal-the-bacon game using hockey sticks and a ball or puck instead of a handkerchief.

Along opposite walls two equal sized teams line up facing into the playing "field" and count off in order, numbering themselves in one direction on one team and in the opposite direction on the other team. Set up a goal at each of the other two ends of the play area using street hockey nets, boxes, or chairs. The object of the game is to score the most goals by hitting the puck or ball into the opponent's net.

Each team is given a hockey stick (a broom will do if you use a larger ball). Team members need to bunch together so that every player can have one hand on the hockey stick. Once play begins all players must

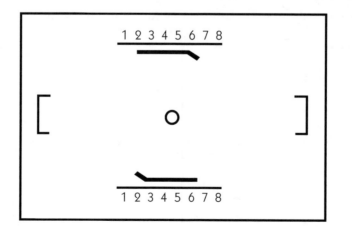

place their other hand on the wall behind them and keep a hand on the wall at all times during the game.

Once everyone is in position with one hand on the wall and one hand holding the stick, call out one of the numbers assigned to the players. The players with that number take their hands off the wall, grab their team's stick, run out to face their opponent in the center of the field, and attempt to make a goal. The rest of the team members release the stick but must keep a hand on the wall. Removing one's hand from the wall costs a player's team one point. When one player scores, both return to their teams and all hold the hockey stick and wait for a new number to be called.

To keep more kids in the game and speed up the pace of play, call for new players before a goal is scored. The two players in the center must then drop their sticks where they are, return to their lines, and put a hand on the wall before the next players can go out. Groups of fifty or more may need to divide up into four teams—one pair with letters and one with numbers. During the game call out numbers and letters alternately.

INDOOR GAMES FOR SMALL GROUPS

Assault II

In a gym or any large area, set up four barriers (tables, desks) to create a course that players must run in order, from start to finish, as quickly as possible, with a one-minute maximum time. The real challenge, however, is that they must run the course without getting hit by the tennis balls being thrown by the "gladiators."

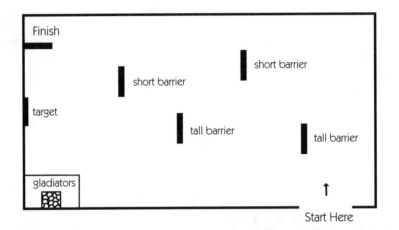

In one corner of the play area, two gladiators armed with a bucket of fifty or more tennis balls fire off shots at players attempting to run the course. Players must wear appropriate safety gear—goggles, head gear, and knee pads are recommended. At a signal a player runs from the start area to each of the barriers in the order shown in the diagram, trying to make the fastest time while avoiding being hit by the flying tennis balls.

As an extra twist, place an eight-foot target on the wall behind the gladiators and plant several tennis balls behind the barriers. When players reach a barrier, they may pick up the tennis ball (or grab a discarded ball on the run) and throw it at the target. Players who hit the target receive a deduction of five seconds off of their time for each time they hit the target with a ball.

Balloon Mini-Golf

To turn your church into a miniature golf course, number boxes and other kinds of containers and lay them out to be the "holes" in a golf course. Run the "fairway" in and out of rooms, down hallways, up stairs, over "water hazards" (the baptistry), and so on. Provide the kids with plastic floor hockey sticks for golf clubs and give players four-inch, round balloons to use as golf balls—to keep the game unpredictable. Players attempt to follow the course, hitting their balls into the prepared holes. To add to the fun, create some adverse "weather" conditions, like placing a fan along one of the fairways. Play the course ahead of time to establish par for each hole.

Balloon Pong

All set up for Ping-Pong, only to find no Ping-Pong balls? Get some balloons and play this slo-mo version of Ping-Pong.

Line your kids up in two lines, one against each end of the Ping-Pong table. Players play according to regular Ping-Pong rules—except that they hit a balloon instead of a ball (weighted with a marble inside, if necessary) and play with a single paddle. After a player hits the balloon, he slides the paddle across the table under the net to the player opposite him—who grabs the paddle (before the balloon arrives) and returns the balloon, Ping-Pong fashion. Once a player makes her shot and slides the paddle to another player, she scoots out of the way to the back of her line as quickly as possible.

Slower players may bend the rules a bit and keep the balloon aloft with their breath if they need time to snatch the paddle.

Banana Duel

Team up your kids in pairs, have partners clasp their hands, then tie those hands together. Give each player a banana with these instructions: players are to peel the banana any way they can (usually with teeth and right hands) before cramming it into their partner's mouth.

If your playing area can take the inevitable mess, enliven the game by blindfolding some or all the players.

Blindman Bacon

This variation of steal the bacon works best when played in a circle. Number off players in two teams of equal size—one player on each team having the same number. Place a loaded squirt gun in the center of the circle, and give each team a blindfold.

When you call a number, the corresponding players put on their blindfolds. At a signal, both players attempt to locate the squirt gun as their teammates scream directions. The player who finds the squirt gun tries to squirt the other player before that player can retreat behind her or his teammates—all this while both of them are still wearing their blindfolds. Players who score a hit against their opponents earn a point for their team. Players who escape a hit from the squirt gun earn the point for their team.

When the kids get good at locating the squirt gun, mix them up by moving it after the blindfolds go on.

Carnival Concentration

For this variation of the TV game show *Concentration*, ask one of the kids with artistic flair to create a concentration-style puzzle to put on a bulletin board. The puzzle could be a common expression, a line from a popular song, the title from a TV show or movie, or a verse of Scripture. Then tape inflated balloons over the entire puzzle using clear tape.

When it's time to play, break the group into two or three teams. Teams take turns throwing darts at the balloons. When a player pops a balloon, that player's team gets fifteen seconds to try to solve the puzzle. A team can only guess the puzzle when one of its members has popped a balloon. The winning team is the first to successfully solve the puzzle.

Double Body Surfing

Ask the kids to take off their shoes, and then form a circle or an oval in the middle of the floor. Have them all lie down on their backs, side by side, with their feet to the center of the circle. Enlist two volunteers—one boy and one girl—to serve as "surfers." Let the group lying on the floor practice rolling to the left and right, all moving in the same direction. Then have the two volunteers lie down across several of the participants with their arms outstretched as if they were about to ride on a really big wave.

On the signal, everyone on the floor begins rolling to the right. At the same time the two volunteers crawl across the rolling players in the same direction. If the group is rolling to the right, for instance, then the two surfers will crawl to the right. The first surfer to make it back to the starting point by crawling across everyone wins.

Dressing in the Dark

To play this game you need piles of activity-specific clothing and blindfolds. Each pile must contain the same type of clothing. On 3 X 5 cards write instructions for which activity players are to dress for, followed by a list of specific clothing to put on. For example, the card reads, "You are going to play tennis. Put on: sweatshirt, socks, tennis shoes, T-shirt." Another card might read, "You are going skiing. Put on: ski jacket, gloves, socks, overalls."

Divide your group into teams of seven or eight, and give to one player from each team the index cards describing the first outfit. After the players have memorized the clothing they are to put on, blindfold them and guide them to their team's pile of clothing. The blindfolded players have three minutes to pull from the pile the correct articles of clothing and dress themselves correctly and neatly—buttons in the correct buttonholes, shirts on inside in, and pants on correctly. The only help the blindfolded players have is their sense of touch and shouted clues from their teammates. At the end of three minutes, if no one is completely dressed, the leader decides who is the best dressed. Otherwise, the player who finishes correctly dressing first earns the point for his or her team.

Driving Range

After a rousing game of "Goofy Golf" (*Play It!*), what could be more natural than a trip to a driving range? Or say, your homemade version of a driving range? Find a room with a high ceiling and try this low-budget thriller. (see diagram on next page)

The advance preparation is simple. Hang on a wall a large piece of butcher paper that goes from ceiling to floor. Draw a series of greens and a water hazard, each with designated points. Try to hit a marshmallow onto one of the greens with a golf club; if you succeed, you get the number of points marked on the green. If you land outside the green, you get the number of points marked in the particular area. If you hit the water hazard, you lose 10,000 points. The person with the highest number of points wins.

Frisbee Bowling

A number of people can play this game, and very little skill is required. To set up, all you need is a table, ten paper cups, and three Frisbees. The cups are stacked in a pyramid several inches away from the far edge of the table. From a distance of about twenty feet, each player gets three attempts to knock as many of the cups as possible onto the floor by hitting them with a Frisbee.

Each cup is worth one point. You can call each round a frame as in regular bowling, with a game consisting of as many frames as you like. If more than five people are playing, keep a pencil and paper handy to keep track of the scores. To keep the game moving, players can take turns throwing the Frisbees, retrieving them, and restacking the paper cups.

Fill My Cup

For this carnival or lock-in game you'll need a table, squirt gun, small cup (an individual communion cup works fine), and a flat, dense surface that can deflect a squirt-gunned stream of water. Anchor the small cup to the table with tape, arrange the deflector behind and above the cup (see diagram), and mark a line behind which shooters must stand. Time the shooters; the winner is the one to fill the cup to the line in the least time. Or set up two targets, and have shooters race each other.

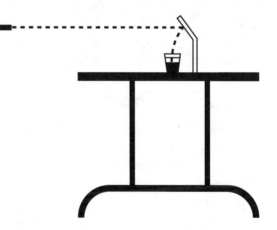

Go Fly a Kite!

For a March fling any time of the year, announce a kite-flying contest, but tell everyone to bring what they need to make a kite—paper, straws,

Popsicle sticks, glue, Scotch tape. (Don't let them bring already-made kites.) The ones the group will fly must be several times smaller than regular kites because they'll be flown with the help of a window fan and some yarn that you'll supply.

Give the kids a set time to create small kites, using whatever material they wish, just so long as the kite can stay up whenever the fan is blown at full blast. The best kites are those made in the traditional diamond shape. After everyone has made a kite, begin tying them to the fan one at a time with about three to four feet of yarn (shorter lengths if the yarn is heavy), and turn the fan on full blast, facing into the center of the room. Add more kites and see how many you can fly without tangling them up together. This activity works well with a small group.

Hidden in Plain Sight

In a relatively cluttered room, hide about twenty small items where players can see them without having to open drawers or move other items. A shoelace can be wrapped around a chair leg, a dollar bill can be folded up and wrapped around a book spine, a pen can be placed atop a door frame with only the end showing, a button can be taped to a doorknob. Write out and photocopy a list of the things you've hidden—pen, a bobby pin, a clothespin, a match—and then place a duplicate of each hidden item on a tray beside the lists.

When the kids are ready to play, give them each a copy of the list of hidden items, and leave the tray of duplicate items out for comparison. Set a time limit for the players to search the room to find each of the listed items. They are not to remove the items; they are only to note the location of each item. The winner is the player who finds the most items within the time limit.

Hovercraft Drag Races

Set out 8 1/2" by 11" sheets of paper, crayons, pencils, or markers. Instruct your students to design their own sports car—a flat, two dimensional dream machine, colored from a bird's-eye view. Encourage them to use their imaginations—to name their cars, cover them with "sponsors" names and logos, number them. Remind them to distinguish the front from the rear.

The drag strip is a table; provide start and finish lines. Owners of the hovercraft dragsters puff lightly on the rear of the vehicles to "float" them down the strip and across the finish line. Leaving the strip (falling off the table) and spin-outs (when the rear of the dragster is farther down the strip than its front) disqualify the "drivers," who can race the clock or each other in time trials and tournaments.

The final race can be the "Hovercraft 500." Set a square race trace with four tables, place some "puffers" on the inside of the track, then have each team race the clock and try to better each others' times.

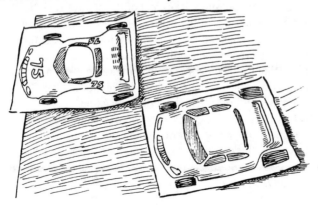

Indoor Frisbee Golf

Go to your local dairy and ask for a donation of thirty or more five-pound cottage cheese lids, or find some lids around the house that are at least six inches in diameter. These are small enough not to break anything, but large enough to be thrown with a degree of accuracy. Number the lids so the kids can tell them apart.

Set up a course ahead of time using trash cans as the "holes." Print up score cards and rules like the ones below. After explaining the rules to the group, start each group at a different location so they can theoretically all start and finish at the same time.

This can be a great spur-of-the-moment-game if you use permanent targets and have your lids and score cards ready.

> Indoor Frisbee Golf
> 1. Golfers should be in groups of two to four players.
> 2. Stay with your group and don't run around wildly.
> 3. At each hole, take turns throwing your first putt.
> 4. Count how many throws it takes to make your putt and write down the score. (Lowest score wins.)
> 5. You may not be farther than three feet from the previous hole when you start throwing to the next.
> 6. You may not stop a Frisbee that is moving or rolling.
> 7. One foot must touch the spot where the Frisbee lands when you throw it (except at the start of each hole).
> 8. Each team decides at the beginning if it will use pro rules (the Frisbee must land inside the trash can) or beginner rules (the Frisbee need only hit the can).
> 9. It is polite for members of a slower team to allow a faster team to pass them. It is not polite for a faster team to interfere with a slower team's game.
> 10. All holes are trash cans except where noted otherwise.
> 11. For simplicity, par is four on all holes (72 total).
> 12. Have fun, but don't destroy the building in the process.

(Score cards on next page)

1 - Kindergarten Room 12
2 - Three-year-old Room 13
3 - Top of the back stairs
   (anywhere on tile floor)
4 - Sacristy Room 109
5 - Acolyte Room 108
6 - Chapel Room 107
7 - Trash can by coat rack
8 - Trash can by phone
9 - Music Room 201

10 - Library Room 2
11 - Second grade Room 3
12 - Nursery Room 4
13 - Fifth/sixth grade Room 5
14 - Fourth grade Room 7
15 - First grade Room 8
16 - Four-year-olds Room 9
17 - Third grade room 10
18 - Youth Room 11

Player / Hole				
1				
2				
3				
4				
5				
6				
7				
8				
9				
Total				

Player / Hole				
10				
11				
12				
13				
14				
15				
16				
17				
18				
1-9				
10-18				
Grand Total				

Jumping Egg Rope

This simple crowd breaker requires three volunteers who are told they'll participate in a rope-jumping contest. Right before they begin competition, announce that contestants will hold an egg between their teeth. As they jump, be sure to push them to go faster. The winner is the one who can jump the longest without cracking or dropping the egg.

Kool-Aid Taste-Off

Ask three volunteers to sit in chairs facing the rest of the group. On a signal they each open a different flavored packet of Kool-Aid. They then lick just one finger and dip it into the packet. The person who in that manner is the first to eat all of the Kool-Aid in the packet wins. It's hilarious because they do not anticipate it being so sour, and they usually end up with it all over their lips.

Lick and Stick

Now it's the girls' turn. In pairs of one boy and one girl, give each girl a pack of Lifesavers—the fruit-flavored ones, not the minty ones. On "go" each girl rips open her pack, then licks them and sticks them to her partner's face. If one falls off, she can pick it up and lick it and stick it on again. First pair to have the entire pack sticking to the boy's face wins. Or give teams a time limit; then if more than one pair gets their entire pack on the boys' faces, judge the winner by how long beyond the time limit the Lifesavers stay stuck to a face.

For the ultimate stickiness, advise the girls to put all the Lifesavers in their mouths at once, then pull them out to stick them on their partners' face.

Masking-Tape Maze

If you have a large room with a clean floor, use masking tape to create a maze on the floor. Then play a regular game of tag with your kids. Players pretend that the wide tape strips represent invisible walls that cannot be crossed, jumped, or reached through. You'll probably want some referees to watch for corner-cutters and wall-climbers, who can be penalized by being made IT.

Musical Pillow Fighting

Similar to the classic game musical chairs, this game uses pillows instead of chairs. Have kids walk around in the dark while you play a music video on the television. When the music stops, kids pick up a pillow and fight until the music comes back on the screen. Remove one pillow with each elimination so that there is always one pillow less than there are players. Continue the game until only a few kids are left.

Musical Sponge

For another musical-chairs type game, set up the same number of chairs as there are players. Blindfold players, who will circle the chairs holding onto the shoulders of the person in front of them. Before the music stops, the leader places a wet sponge on one of the chairs. The unfortunate player who sits on the wet sponge when the music stops (or when the whistle blows) is out. Remove a chair with each player eliminated.

Neckloose

Here's a contest suitable for almost any thematic event, whether it's a Hawaiian luau, a western round-up, or a sweetheart banquet. The only item used in this event is a necklace (of sorts), which can be a plastic lei (for a luau), an old necktie (for a hobo party), or a string of candy hearts (for a sweetheart banquet).

Begin by having everyone make a loose circle, alternating boy-girl-boy-girl. Place the necklace around one neck and instruct participants that on the signal the necklace is to be passed around the circle in the following way: the person beside the one wearing the necklace places his or her head inside the necklace—which is still around the first player's neck—and, without using hands, carefully removes it from the original wearer without breaking or tearing it in any way.

The necklace should be large enough to make the game comfortable, but small enough to make it a challenge. For added fun, start two necklaces in opposite directions and see what happens when they meet in the middle.

Obstacle Ball

When a sudden rain shower threatens to dampen your recreation spirit, retreat indoors to a large room (or even a small fellowship hall) with a foam bat and ball (available in most discount variety stores). Divide the group into two teams.

Now for the wrinkle. Leaving a clear running lane between home plate and first base, litter the "field" liberally with folding chairs—this way a hit ball will ricochet off or roll under a chair where it's hard to get to. Throws to put out runners will be deflected. And when the shower passes, you can move the game outside, too.

Oddball Crawl

Begin this relay by creating two or more teams of eight to ten players wearing their grubbies. At one end of a long room, line up the teams alternating boy-girl-boy-girl on each team. In each line players get on their hands and knees side by side on the floor. On the signal, the players at the end of each team's line closest to the wall begin crawling over and under their teammates as fast as possible. The stationary players alternately drop to the floor or arch up their backs (still keeping hands and feet on the floor) to make passage quicker for their traveling team member.

As soon as possible after the first players have crossed the second players, the second players may begin their trip over and under the stationary teammates. When traveling players reach the end of the line, they either lie flat or rise to allow other players to pass over or under them. The relay continues until everyone on the team has successfully crawled over and under the rest of the team. The team that completes the relay first is the winner.

If your group is too small for two teams, form one team and play several rounds to go for the fastest team time. Have a camera handy to catch some of the action.

Awkward personal contact is rare, for the youths are sufficiently caught up in the race that they don't take time for mischief.

Office Party

Here's a wild game that requires a rubber playground ball and a rotating office chair on wheels. Have the kids form a circle with the chair in the middle. A player sits on the chair while the kids in the circle try to hit the chair with the ball. The player on the chair tries to protect the chair by rolling around on the chair, spinning around, and deflecting the throws. Use your imagination to keep the game going—the player throwing a ball that hits the chair must take his or her place in the chair; when the chair is hit, the youngest member goes to the chair, the newest member, the one wearing school colors.

Pass Out

Based on the faithful standby game *Pass the Lifesaver*, Pass Out is sure to frustrate players—that is, until they figure out the knack to it.

Divide the group into teams of eight to sixteen players and line them up as if for *Pass the Lifesaver*. Give everyone a toothpick. At one end of each line, have ready a Lifesaver, a Kleenex, a seedless grape, and a piece of yarn or string. Team members are to pass all four items from one end of their line to the other.

But don't wait too long before starting the next item, because that's when the fun begins—the middle players get stymied trying to figure out how, with a grape bayonetted on the end of their toothpicks, to pass the Lifesaver; or how to pass a piece of yarn if a Kleenex is draped over their toothpicks.

Here's the secret: Let's take the worst-case scenario and say all four things pile up on a single person in the middle of the line who has to pass them all in their correct order. First the player takes the Lifesaver (sliding it far back on the toothpick), then impales the grape, then grabs the Kleenex with the corner of his or her mouth (aha!), then hangs the yarn on top of everything.

To unload it all, he or she passes the Kleenex one way, turns and lets another have the yarn, passes the grape off in the direction of its destination, and ditto for the Lifesaver. Voila!

Ping Bag

Several early-bird students in a youth group came up with this idea for passing time while waiting for slower groups to finish a discussion question. Every player has a Ping-Pong paddle to toss and catch a small bean bag. You can toss the bag to anyone in the circle—it's every man for himself. If players miss the bean bag, they're out. If the toss is determined by group consensus to be uncatchable, the tosser is out. The trick is to toss the bag so that it's difficult to catch but still possible for an aggressive player. When only one player is left in the circle, everyone joins the circle and round two begins.

Pop Fly! Ground Ball!

The object of this indoor game for about twenty-four players is to be the first of four teams to successfully throw or roll a colored Nerf ball among all its members and then back to the captain.

First, arrange the chairs in a square, divide the group into four equal teams, and instruct members of each team to sit opposite their teammates.

Next, give each team a different-colored Nerf ball. Volunteer one person on each team to be captain; the four captains should sit at one of the ends of their team and should sit in the same positions relative to their teams.

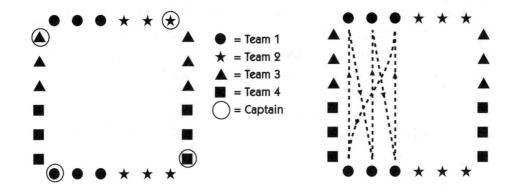

● = Team 1
★ = Team 2
▲ = Team 3
■ = Team 4
○ = Captain

Here's how the game is played. Each captain tosses the team's Nerf ball across the square to a teammate opposite him or her. That player then tosses the ball back across the square to the player seated next to the captain—and so on. You can imagine the delightful chaos of four teams of teenagers all trying to pass Nerf balls through the same confined area. The last person on the team to receive the ball tosses it back to the captain, after which all the team members stand up and yell—thus letting everyone else know they've finished.

Now here's what makes it more fun—at any time, the leader can yell "Ground ball!" At this signal all teams must immediately begin rolling their balls across the floor instead of throwing them. And when they hear "Pop fly!" they return to tossing the balls. It's illegal for the leader to yell the same signal several times in succession—just to keep the kids guessing!

Popsicle Stick Frisbee

With a large supply of Popsicle sticks, teams can make "flying Frisbees" by arranging them according to the diagram. A frisbee can be made with twelve Popsicle sticks.

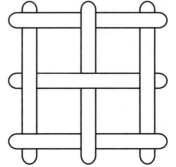

After the kids have had a chance to make their Frisbees, play Frisbee toss games with them (for accuracy and distance). The only Frisbees that score points are those that land without falling apart.

Q-Tip War

Divide your groups into two teams separated by a line down the middle of the play area. Give each team member a straw and five to ten Q-Tips and let them open fire! Players blow-gun as many Q-tips as possible across the line onto the enemy's side of the room before time runs out. Players can reload with Q-Tips shot over onto their side.

After shooting ends, objective volunteers count the Q-Tips on each side. The team with fewer Q-Tips on its side wins.

Shooting Gallery

Blindfold several adult leaders and give them kazoos or party noisemakers. They are the "ducks" in this shooting gallery, moving back and forth and bobbing up and down behind a wall or board that's five feet high or so, "quacking" all the while.

From about ten feet away, kids have five throws of a beach ball to hit the "ducks." Most hits wins; carnival-type prizes are appropriate.

Rollerball

All players lie down on the floor in two lines, side by side with teammates and toe to toe with the other team. Ask players in one line to raise their legs perpendicular to the floor while the players in the other line scoot toward them, raising their legs also until the back sides of the legs of both teams are almost touching each other. On the signal, the pair at one end of the line passes a Nerf ball to the next pair using only their feet. The object is to pass the ball from one end of the line to the other and back again, using only the feet. Play several rounds so the players can get the hang of working with each other to keep the ball from hitting the floor or falling off the line.

Snoot Shoot

The idea of the game is to see how far players can propel Kix, Cheerios, or other bits of breakfast cereals across the room—using the air from their noses!

To play, mark out a line behind which players must stand. They must then place the Kix, for instance, in one nostril of their choice. On the word "fire," while holding the other nostril shut, they must exhale through their noses with as much force as possible, blowing the cereal across the room. Furthest distance wins.

Use this as a crowd breaker or as one event in a series of relays or target-shooting contests, with each team choosing a representative to compete.

Spell My Feet

The object of this hilarious game is for players to form words as quickly as they can. Two teams of five members each sit facing the audience. Using a large black marker, the leaders inscribe letters on the soles of the feet of the players. The first player on each team gets an A on one foot and an N on the other; the second receives an E and a T; the third, G and R; the fourth, O and M; the fifth, S and P.

The leader then calls out a word, and the group that is able to line up their feet to spell that word in the shortest amount of time wins that particular round.

Easy words, worth five points each: master, roast, smear, togas, snore.

More difficult phrases, worth ten points each: ten proms, get Spam, great son, more naps.

The last series, worth twenty points per word, requires teams to compose their own words—the team using the most letters to form a word or combination of words wins the round.

States

Everyone sits in a circle and takes the name of a state (Tennessee, Oregon, and so on). One person chosen to begin the game stands in the middle of the circle with a rolled-up newspaper. When the newspaper-wielder calls out the name of a state, the person who represents that state must stand up and call out the name of another state before the newspaper-wielder can whack him on the head with the newspaper. The round continues until the whacker in the center actually whacks a state-person on the head before the latter calls out another state. The whackee then becomes the whacker, and accordingly takes his or her place in the center, rolled newspaper in hand.

Just a few guidelines:

• You must call the name of a state that's represented in the group.

- You cannot call the state that just called you.
- You cannot call the state of the person in the middle.

Action can get fast and furious between just a few states, so occasionally redistribute the states among the players so that everyone participates.

Strobe Ball

Try playing the old familiar four-square or volleyball in a room lit only by a strobe light (available at electronics shops). It's surprising how difficult it becomes to keep a semblance of coordination. Kids will be swinging at balls and usually missing.

Swinging Marshmallow

Pair up the kids (player A and player B) and give each pair a four-foot-long piece of string and two marshmallows. At a signal the pairs tie one marshmallow on each end of the string. Player A in each pair holds one marshmallow in her mouth while standing facing the front of the room. Player B stands to the side of player A at an arm's length, looking toward player A.

Moving only her head, player A begins to swing the string back and forth like a pendulum while player B attempts to catch the swinging marshmallow in his mouth. Player B may move only his head. The winner is the first pair in which player B catches the marshmallow.

Team Nintendo

Borrow or rent a big screen TV and the latest Nintendo offering for two teams of kids to battle for the video-game championship.

Start the game with one person from each team at the controls and the rest of the team standing ten feet behind the players. Players have thirty seconds at the controls—you manage the stopwatch—while their teams cheer them on. After thirty seconds the next two players run up to the controls and take over, hopefully without missing a shot. When all members of the team have taken their turn playing, round one is over and the score is recorded.

Play as long as enthusiasm lasts and promise a stupendous prize to the team with the most points.

Tic-Tac-Dart

On a large bulletin board, stick strips of masking tape in order to form a big tic-tac-toe figure with eighteen-inch squares. Tape three or four inflated balloons inside each of the nine squares.

Divide your group into two teams. A player from the first team throws a single dart, trying to pop a balloon. If she succeeds, the next in line from her team attempts to pop another; if she fails, the other team sends a thrower to the line to try. The catch is this: whichever team pops the last balloon in a square claims that square with an X or O.

You don't need darts, either—lay out the tic-tac-toe design and balloons on the floor, and drop sharpened pencils on them to pop them.

Toilet Bowl

Sequel to the *Cereal Bowl* and the *Super Bowl*, Toilet Bowl requires minimal set-up: Construct one or two toilet seat-and-lid combinations from heavy cardboard (better yet, use real toilet seats), prop them open so that the open lids serve as backboards, distribute a Scotch-taped roll of toilet paper to each team, and make up some simple rules for a game whose object is to toss the toilet-paper "football" into the "toilet."

You might design a free-throw game in tournament fashion, using a chart on which teams can see who advances to the finals.

Turnover

Form two teams of six players each (more are okay, but no fewer than four players on a team). Using a volleyball and regulation net and court, play volleyball, but with this difference—the player whose mistake gives the team the serve or a point will be turned over to play on the opposing team's side.

It gets heroic as one team dwindles to two or even one player who must stand ten or eleven opponents.

Wacky Balloon

Place a ball of Silly Putty inside a seven-inch balloon and partially blow up the balloon. Clip the knot off as close as possible and you've got a durable balloon that moves in swirls. Now play volley-pong on a Ping-Pong table, using hands instead of paddles to hit the balloon. Except when players serve or return the serve, they must make the balloon bounce on the opponents' side before it can be returned. Place teams of two on either end of the table. Play to five, and then trade teams so everyone gets to play.

You can also use the wacky balloon and a plastic whiffle bat to play indoor baseball. The pitchers can get the Silly Putty whirling around the inside of the balloon before they pitch the ball. Or during the teaching time, toss the balloon to indicate who must answer one of the questions.

RELAYS

Adam and Eve Relay

Arrange boy-girl pairs in typical relay teams. The object is for a pair to sink their teeth into an apple and walk it to their teammates across the room. They must pass the apple to the new boy-girl pair without hands—their teammates must bite into it while the first pair are still holding it in their teeth. (Smaller apples make this maneuver hilarious.) No hands permitted except to pick up a dropped apple.

Balloon Balance Relay

Form teams and give each team one baseball cap or painter's cap. The first player from each team dons the cap and balances an inflated balloon on the bill (bouncing on the bill is permitted). The players then walk to a point ten feet away and back again while balancing the balloon on their hats. Then, using their hands, they pass the balloon and hat to the next players in line, who do the same thing.

A player whose balloon falls to the floor or is held up by any part of the body has to start over. (No fair blowing on the balloon to keep it in place.) The first team whose players all complete the circuit is declared the uncontested balloon balance relay champions of the world.

Balloon Bomb Dress-Up Relay

For this relay, each team needs a dress-up box with the same number and kinds of objects—old coat, gloves, hat, scarf, boots. As teammates take their turns racing to the box and then dressing and undressing with the old clothes, they must keep a balloon in the air. If the balloon touches the ground, they must start their dressing over again.

Buckle Up Relay

You'll need one bench seat per team for this game (the van variety, with seat belts attached); the removable seats from mini-vans work fine. Place the bench seats at a starting line. At a designated distance mark a finish line. Divide the kids into two (or more) groups. Place half of each team at the starting line and the other half at the finish line.

Instruct the first three of each team at the starting line to belt themselves into the van seats. On "go" the three belted-in players of each team stand to their feet and lumber toward the finish line, lugging the bench seat with them. When they arrive at the far line, they set the seat down, release the seat belts, and the second set of three strap themselves in and race back. Play continues until one team wins when its final racers release the seat belts.

Bump Relay

Teams of ten or so are seated in a line of chairs lined up relay fashion. At a signal, the first players in each line leave their seats and rush along the right side to the back of their lines, then—with some adept hip action— "bump" the teammates off their chairs to the right (see diagram at right). The bumped

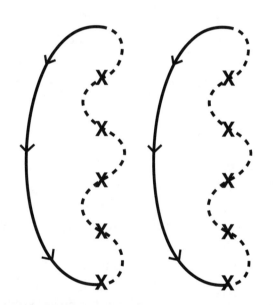

ones move forward a chair and bump those teammates off to the left—and so on to the players one chair behind the front of the line. The last players bumped must sit down briefly in the front chair before running around to the rear of their lines and starting the process over again.

First team's players to return to their original chairs wins.

Bunny Buster

Play this relay with small party balloons and teams of ten—five girls and five boys. The boys on each team line up on one side of the room, while the girls line up about thirty-five feet away on the other side of the room. The first boy in each team is handed a balloon, which he must inflate as quickly as possible without stretching it first. Once he's blown it up, he carries it in his mouth, without using his hands, to the girl opposite him. She removes it from his mouth with her hands, not letting any air out, and holds it on the floor without tying it. The boy must then sit on the balloon and break it. Once he breaks it, he runs back and tags the next boy in line, and the cycle starts over. Not only is it hilarious watching the boys try to blow up the balloons without stretching them, but sometimes the balloon escapes as they race to the girls or the now slobbery end of the balloon slops out of the girls' fingers or the boy smashes the girl's hand when he tries to pop the balloon or.... Well, you try it!

Cake Relay

Ideal for a camp or a retreat, this relay sends each teammate on a different leg of this relay, passing not a baton from runner to runner, but a store-bought pound cake on a paper plate (or even Twinkies or melons).

The first leg of the relay is an obstacle course; the second, a walking foot race (those who run are penalized by having to stand still for fifteen seconds); the third, a swim across the pool or waterfront keeping the cake above water; for the fourth leg the runner is blindfolded and directed verbally from the starting line to the finish line by a partner; the final leg of the relay is an all-out sprint for a quarter-mile or so.

When their last teammate crosses the finish line, team members must eat the cake. After all the wear and tear the cakes have endured—being dropped, soaked, manhandled—the climax is hilarious. A great group builder, this game requires teamwork and can be adapted to various situations.

Centipede Relay

Form equal teams of six or eight kids each and line up, alternating boy-girl-boy-girl. Instruct teams to back up to the wall at one end of the room, leaving three to four feet between the last person and the wall.

On a signal each team must take three short steps forward. As soon as the team has moved forward the last step, the first players in the lines break away to the right and run around their team three times as fast as possible, finally taking their place at the back of their team's line. Once in place, the runner yells, "Go!" and the process repeats with three more steps and a new front runner.

The relay continues until the line itself arrives at the youth leader standing at the other end of the room, or until a team crosses a line drawn on the floor.

(The room need not be large, since teams don't need that much room to move forward. They mainly need room on the sides of the lines to run around their teams without bumping into the competition. For every three steps forward, the team loses one-body space backward as the runner takes his place at the end of the line.)

As a true test of speed and skill, runners attempt to circle their team faster and faster. The key to winning this relay, however, is for all players to press as close as possible to the people in front of and behind them. To make each line tighter, instruct players to grasp hold of the waist of the one standing directly in front of them. (The kids may feel awkward doing this at first, but they'll comply as soon as they see their team losing the race.)

Be sure to point out that each person on the team may have to run several times before the entire team reaches the marker at the other end of the room. Also point out that the three short steps must be short. Demonstrate how they can move forward by simply placing one foot directly in front of the other, toe to heel, and moving.

Chewing Gum Relay

Start with a few packs of wrapped chewing gum and a pair of work gloves and a shopping bag for each team. Place individual sticks of gum (wrapped) inside the shopping bags and give each team a pair of work gloves. Players must put on the gloves, run to the bag, pull out a piece of gum, unwrap it (with the gloves on), chew it, and then run back to pass the gloves to the next person of their team. Repeat the process until everyone on the team is chewing gum. The team that finishes first is the winner.

Connect Four

Divide a large group into teams of five or six pairs, or ask the entire group to form a line of pairs. The first pair places a rubber playground ball between them at stomach level. To help keep the ball from falling and to help maintain balance, the two players place their hands on each others' shoulders. At a signal the next pair in line, in the same stance, tries to get the ball from the first pair—not with their hands, but by securing the ball between them at the stomach (see diagram below). The object is to pass the ball as quickly as possible from one set of people to the next without letting it fall.

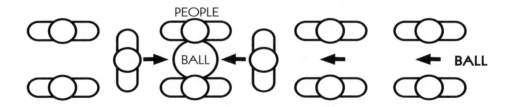

Dough-Tongue Shuffle

Divide the group into two equal-sized teams in which players line up one behind the other. Give the first player in each line a large donut (preferably plain). On a signal those players must tilt their heads back, hold their donuts by sticking their tongues through the donut hole, and run up to and around a given obstacle without dropping the donut—no hands allowed. After running around the obstacle, the runners take their donuts in their hands, race to a waiting judge, and completely eat their donuts (to the satisfaction of the judge). Then the judge gives runners another donut, which they carry in their hands back to their team and place on the tongue of the next person in the relay line. The relay continues in the same way. The first team to complete the relay by running all its members shouts "The Dough-Tongue Shuffle!" and wins.

Fruit Basket Fly-By

For each team, place one fruit-filled basket at one end of a large room and a second empty basket at the other end of the room. Across the middle of the room, set up a barrier of chairs or tables. Teams compete to see who can be first to transfer all the fruit from their full basket into their empty one. The challenge is that the fruit can only be transported by "fruit flies," whose teammates carry them aloft and over the barrier.

To play, half of each team's players stand by their team's full basket and the other half by the empty one. On a signal, players near their team's full basket pick one among their group to become the fruit fly. Fruit flies tuck a piece of fruit under their chins, hold their arms out like wings, and are carried by their teammates up to the barrier. Meanwhile, the corresponding team members near the empty basket approach the far side of the barrier and prepare to receive the fly, who is carefully passed over the barrier. (After passing the fly over, carriers can crawl under or climb over the barrier to help carry the fly on the other side as well.)

Teammates then carry the fly to the empty basket, into which the fly drops the piece of fruit. The fly is let down, and the players who crossed the barrier to assist must run back to the full basket and transport to the "empty" basket the newly chosen fruit fly carrying another piece of fruit. The game continues in this way until all the fruit has been transported.

If necessary, after all players have served as flies, some can repeat the role. If a piece of fruit is dropped en route, the fly must "land," pick it up, tuck it under his or her chin, and take off again as before. The team to complete the task first is the winner.

Golf Ball and Plunger Cap Relay

Have the camera ready for this game! Make two teams and give a plunger (a plumber's helper) and a golf ball to each team. Ask the first players on each team to unscrew the wooden stick from the plunger, place the golf ball where the stick screwed in, and settle the plunger cap on their heads.

Players in this relay now must walk a prescribed course with the plunger cap on their heads and the golf ball balanced on the plunger cap. (The course can be simple—out ten or twenty feet, around a chair, and back, for example.) Players who drop the ball return to their line and start over. For more of a challenge, place obstacles in the course, or make the kids walk it backward.

Indoor Obstacle Course

Form teams limited to six players or less because of the time necessary to complete the obstacle course.

Set up the course as shown in the diagram on the next page. Each player is given a soda straw. On the signal, one player from each team goes to the starting position to pick up one of five kernels of corn from a paper plate. The only way players can move the corn, however, is by sucking on the straw and creating a vacuum that holds the kernel while they walk over to a foam cup on the near side of a table five feet away. Once they reach the cup, they drop the kernel in it and go back for the next one, continuing until all the kernels have been moved. If a kernel is dropped en route, the player may pick it up again (using the same method) and continue.

Once all five kernels are in the cup, players must blow the cup across the table (the wider the table, the better) and make it land in a box placed on the floor underneath the table's far edge. If the cup or any of the corn misses the box, the cup must be refilled by a designated assistant from the player's team and then replaced on the table's edge. The player keeps trying until the cup and corn all fall into the box at once.

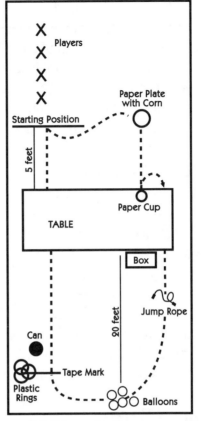

Next, players crawl under the table, grab a jump rope on the other side, and jump with it over to a spot twenty feet away, where a pile of uninflated balloons is waiting. They must blow up one balloon till it bursts, then run to a tape mark on the floor five feet away (see the diagram). There they must pick up two plastic rings from the floor and toss them around a can three feet away. (Empty bread crumb cans work well for this.) When the players have made a successful toss with both rings, they crawl back under the table and tag the next person (and probably collapse). The first team to complete the relay wins.

The game is as much fun to watch as it is to play, so kids who don't want to run the course may enjoy acting as assistants. Besides helping out with unsuccessful cup-blowing attempts, the assistants must also replace the cup on the table and the corn on the plate after the player has succeeded in that part of the relay.

As a variation you can use a stopwatch and allow individual players to compete against the clock.

Long-Jump Relay

Divide contestants into teams of six or eight, mark a starting line, and have kids stand by teams in single file behind it.

At the signal to go, each leader does a standing broad jump straight ahead—both feet must leave the ground simultaneously. The next player in line then runs up to him, places his feet exactly where the leader's feet are, and does another standing broad jump. The third player runs up to the second and repeats the process. Likewise, each player in turn rushes forward and jumps from where the preceding player landed.

After the last player of every team has jumped, the total distance of each team is measured, and the farthest distance wins.

Mummy Race

This relay requires teams to wrap up a teammate completely in sheet strips and then carry the "mummies" up to the line and back. Each teammate is so wrapped and toted. First crypt of mummies finished with this sepulchral task wins.

Pyramids by Braille

In this relay blindfolded players must crawl ten or twenty feet in front of their teams to where six Styrofoam cups lie. They must stack up their set of six, pyramid fashion, before returning to their teams and passing the blindfold off to a teammate. You, meanwhile, knock down each pyramid for the next players.

Q-Tip Shuffle

This game may leave the taste of cotton in kids' mouths, but it's fun!

Form teams of ten or less. Place one person from each team about thirty feet ahead of the rest of the team. The first players on each team place up to ten Q-Tips in various parts of their body (ears, nose, mouth, hair, crook of arms, pockets, shoes). They cannot carry any Q-Tips with their hands.

Then they shuffle ahead to their teammates, trying not to drop any Q-Tips. Their teammates must then dislodge the Q-Tips with their teeth and drop them into their team's pile. The "biter" then runs back to the rest of the team and tags the next person in line, who already has his or her Q-Tips placed and is ready to do the shuffle. The first carrier stays at the Q-Tip pile and becomes the next "biter."

The relay continues until all the members of one team have completed the relay, shuffling their team to victory.

Retread Regatta

Get some bald tires, slice them in half like a bagel, fill each half with water, and—voila—your own Ping-Pong-ball regatta courses! Give each team its own water-filled tire, mark starting points with chalk, and begin the race. Each team member must take turns blowing the Ping-Pong ball once around the course. First team in which every member rounds the tire wins.

Variations: Use sand instead of water; blindfold players so that they depend on their teammates' directions; invent your own games.

School Craze

This relay race is a back-to-school event. Two teams race each other through a battery of school-like tasks, each teammate responsible for one leg of the relay. Set up a large room with the necessary equipment and furniture (see diagram). Assign one member of each team to each of the stations that form the relay course.

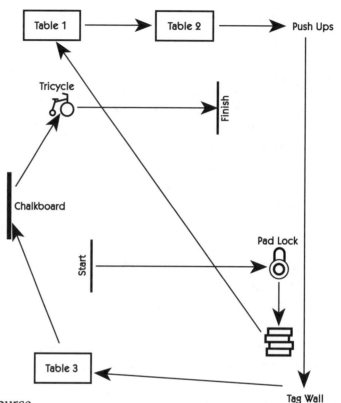

1. At the sound of the tardy bell, the team members at the starting line sprint across the room, open a combination lock (the combination is written on a piece of paper taped to the lock), then tag the second members of their teams, who are waiting by the large stack of books.

2. When tagged, teammate two picks up the books (make it challenging, but don't cause any hernias) and, stooping to retrieve any that he or she drops, staggers across to table 1.

3. Once the books are plopped down, the third member may turn over a paper on which is printed a maze. When the maze is completed, the teammate takes the maze to table 2, where a "teacher" (a sponsor) corrects it.

4. If the maze passes the scrutiny of the grader, the next teammate performs five push-ups, then races to tag the opposite wall before sprinting to table 3 (this is PE).

5. Now it's lunchtime. When the sprinter arrives at table 3, the fifth member waiting there must consume a burger and a small Coke before dashing to the chalkboard and tagging the sixth teammate.

6. At the board, this member first solves a math problem previously written but covered until now, then copies a short phrase like "More homework!" or "Biology's great!" (for composition) before racing to the next and final teammate waiting on a tricycle.

7. Time to go home. When the tricycle rider is tagged, he or she pedals like mad for the finish line across the room.

Shirt-Button Relay

The object of this relay is (have you guessed yet?) to run up to a shirt (for more, uh, interest, the shirt can be on the male youth leader) and unbutton it. The next player must then re-button it, and so on through the line of players.

Shovel Trouble

Shovel in hand, the first player in each team skateboards to a common pile of spuds at the other end of the lot, shovels up one potato, skates back to his team, deposits the potato in his team's box or basket, then passes both shovel and skateboard to the next teammate, who follows suit.

The game continues as long as the taters last; when they're gone, teams count what they've collected. The team with the most wins. Long-handled shovels work better than those with short handles—but the short-handled ones are more of a challenge to work with.

Ski-lays

Okay, so your church is in Mobile or Austin or Gila Bend, and half your group hasn't seen snow, not to mention played or skied in it. But don't let that stop you. Let the Denver and Seattle churches have their ski re-treats—you can play these ski-lays (that's "ski relays") in your own Sun Belt gymnasium or youth room. Make skis from six foot (or longer) boards, and nail old Salvation Army shoes to them. Let these three snow-less ski-lays start you off.

• **Ski Fill.** At the starting line set up a small bucket of water for each team. At the opposite end of the room place a turn-around cone as well as an empty container. Give the first member of each team a paper or Styrofoam cup with a small hole in the bottom. On "go" the players must strap on their skis, fill their leaky cups from the bucket, then ski their way to the cone, where they pour what remains of their water into the container. After they ski back to their own teams, the following players do likewise until one team's container is filled with water.

• **Ski Plunger Toss**. Seat a victim at the far end of the room from the relay starting line. The first player in each team must strap on skis, pick up a plunger by the handle, grab a water balloon from a pile near each team, place the balloon in the plunger end, ski to a designated firing spot, and let fly at the victim (who, in all fairness to the shooters, must sit on his or her hands). Any skier who drops a water balloon en route forfeits his shot and instead returns to his line to let the next teammate go. The winning team is determined however you like—the first to wet the victim, the most hits in the least time.

This game is appropriate for "honoring" a special adult or student. And you may find that most of the balloons don't have enough velocity to pop when they hit the victim. But don't tell the victims that—let them sweat it out.

• **Balloon Racquet Relay**. The object of this relay is to ski the length of the course (either around the cone or through an obstacle course), all the while keeping a balloon in the air with a racquet (tennis, badminton, racquetball). Make whatever variations fit your room or group.

Square-Off Relay

This race is pure frantic confusion. Once you have separate teams, divide each team into groups of four or five and arrange them like the diagram to the right. For fewer players, shape teams in a triangle. The center of the playing area becomes Grand Central Station as players, when their turns come, don't simply run parallel to each other to tag their teammates across the way, but in a

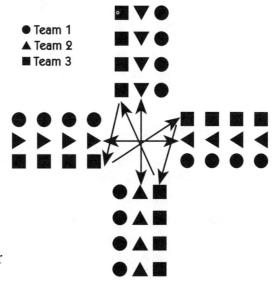

● Team 1
▲ Team 2
■ Team 3

pattern that forces them to cross and recross each others' paths. This one's great for collisions, confusion, and laughs as kids end up in the wrong team lines without realizing it.

Sticky-Buns

For this game ask the kids to line up in pairs behind a line on one side of the room. On the other side of the room spread inflated balloons across the floor. Give each team of two a roll of masking tape, and tell the kids that on "go" they are to apply the tape around the midsection of the person whose birthday is closest to today. The pair must use the whole roll of tape and it must be on sticky-side out.

When the tape is used up, the taped players must crab-walk to the balloons and bring back to their partners waiting at the starting line as many balloons as they can carry without using their hands. The waiting partners must then burst the balloons and save the ring part of the balloon (where you blow it up) to verify the number of balloons retrieved. Balloons popped by the sticky-bunned teammate don't count. The pair with the most rings wins.

This is a game to videotape. The kids are so dizzy from spinning around to get the tape on that they have a hard time doing the rest of the relay.

Superhero Relay

Here's a game you can play next time you're doing a lesson on heroes. You'll need two "phone booths" (be creative; a couple of refrigerator boxes will work); two dolls; several tables; two masks; and two pairs of high-topped tennis shoes.

Divide the group into two teams. Line them up about fifty feet away from the phone booths. The first players from each team race each

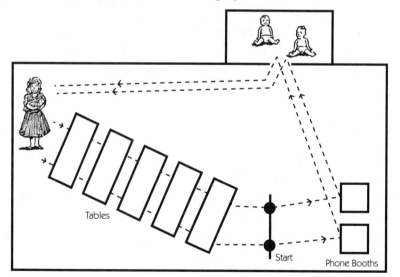

Tables

Start

Phone Booths

other through the course. They first enter the appropriate team phone booth and put on the mask and the "super-powered" shoes. Once dressed a player runs to another room to save a baby (a doll) from a burning building. Next the superhero takes the baby to the hysterical mother back in the other room. Then the superhero recites the "Pledge of Allegiance," standing tall with hand over heart, while the mother hums a patriotic tune.

From there, the superhero tunnels under the earth (crawls under tables) and "flies" back to the phone booth. (This is done by having four people carry each contestant in the flying position.) Finally, the superhero changes back into street clothes and, leaving the mask and shoes in the phone booth, runs back to tag the next player in line, who must run the same course. (Dolls must be returned immediately to the other room.) The first team to finish is the winner.

Tapehead

Whether you play this game as a relay or a watch-and-cheer game, it's hilarious! Students wrap up their partner's head completely with masking tape, sticky side out. Then, in competition, the partial mummies run or crawl to an area where a variety of small, light objects are spread. They must lower their heads onto objects, "stick" 'em, then bring them back to where their partners remove the items and send their mummies back for another trip. The pair or team whose tapehead fetches the most items in a given amount of time wins.

Here are some common articles easily picked up by tapeheads: egg cartons, Styrofoam cups, plastic ware, milk cartons, construction paper, shoe boxes, string, pie tins, paper clips, rubber bands, cotton balls, marshmallows, small stuffed animals, pencils, Q-Tips, inflated balloons, paper plates. To avoid tangling hair in the masking tape, have "tapeheads" put a nylon stocking over their heads first. Then apply the tape.

Whisper the Flavor

Using a package of assorted hard candy or jelly beans with a large variety of flavors, test the taste discrimination of your kids with this relay. Divide into as many teams as necessary. Appoint a member of each team to serve as his or her team's "distributor"—that person should know the flavor of whatever piece of candy is being handed out.

Teams line up in a column, and on signal the person at the front of each team (the runner) runs to the distributor (who is stationed about ten feet away) and receives a piece of candy. The runner then returns to the next person in line (the eater) and puts the candy in that person's mouth. As soon as the eater recognizes the flavor, he or she whispers the flavor to the runner who then runs back to the distributor and whispers the flavor to him or her. (Note: If all distributors give out the same flavors of candy at the same time, one runner could hear the guess of another team's runner and cheat by guessing the same flavor. Thus, whispering is essential!)

If the eater incorrectly guesses the flavor, the runner returns to the eater for another guess, then returns to the distributor, repeating this as many times as necessary until the correct flavor is guessed.

If the eater correctly guesses the flavor, the runner will return to the end of the line, and play continues as before with the previous eater now serving as runner, and the next person in line serving as eater. The team to return its initial runner to the front of the line is the winner.

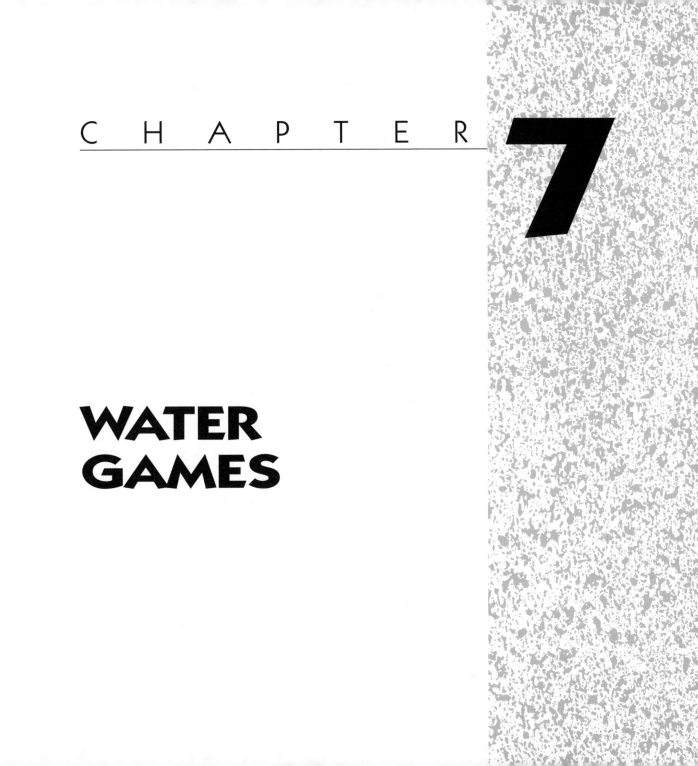

C H A P T E R **7**

WATER
GAMES

Busted

Every group has at least some kids who would burst water balloons over their heads if they knew that a five-dollar bill was in one of the balloons. So on a hot day, give your group a hilarious show, make someone five dollars richer—and maybe pull an object lesson from the silliness (what people will do for money, paying a price for getting what one really wants). Give volunteers only seven seconds; let more volunteers try their luck until the money is found.

Fizzler Tag

Before you play this summertime, laser-tag-type outdoor game, drill a small hole in the center of as many Alka-Seltzer tablets as you have kids, and then run a string through each tablet in order to hang it loosely around a player's neck. Have each player bring a squirt gun, provide several full buckets of water out-of-bounds for refills, and begin the game.

The object? When a player's Alka-Seltzer tablet gets hit enough and dissolves sufficiently to drop off the string, that player is out. To shorten the game, bring out the garden hose!

Firefighter Water Wars

Add this to your list of outdoor, hot-weather water games. You'll need the cooperation of your local fire department, because the game requires a garden-hose adapter to a fire hydrant (fire departments have them). Or else hook up your hoses to your normal water spigots if the water pressure is sufficient for this game.

Use the adapter to hook up three hoses, and suspend an empty paint can on a pulley hanging from a wire or clothesline. Two teams will each use the water stream from their hoses to move an empty paint can toward the opposing team's end. Of course both teams will have an immensely fun and soaking time of it. Form teams and conduct a tournament. (see diagram on next page)

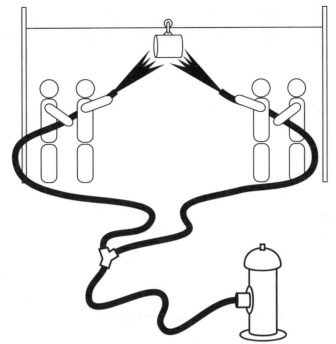

Fling 'Em

Divide lots of water balloons equally between four teams, and send each team to one of the corners in the playing area (see diagram on next page). Each team selects two people to be its "catchers," who take a garbage can with them into the catchers' area. When the game begins, teams attempt to lob their water balloons from their corners to their own catchers' garbage can in the middle of the playing area. The team with the most water in its can when all balloons are gone wins.

Remember these rules:
- Both catchers must hold the garbage can.
- Catcher can catch balloons from any team.
- No physical contact between opposing catchers is permitted unless they're vying for tossed balloons.
- Catchers cannot step out of their designated area.

Devise various ways of propelling the balloons to the cans: sling-shots made from surgical tubing, plastic throwers shaped like those used in jai alai.

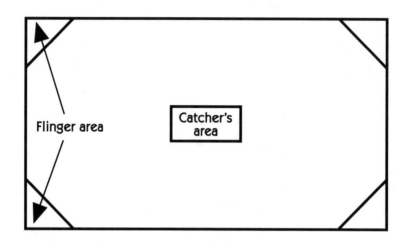

Giant Slip 'n' Slide Relays

With a 20' by 100' sheet of six-mil plastic and a large, smooth grassy area, you're ready for fun! Spread out the plastic, hose it down, add some baby shampoo to make it slick, and maybe some sprinklers along the sides to keep it wet.

Then start the relays: Team members must "swim" from end to end, be dragged by teammates (by hands or feet), or—the messiest of all—the watermelon relay. As racers run the course with a watermelon in their arms, opposing team members pelt them with water balloons—as if the slippery plastic is not obstacle enough. When people drop their watermelons, they must pick up the pieces and continue the race.

When the inevitable free-for-all occurs, forbid the throwing of watermelon pieces (but not the stuffing of them in another's face); and free-for-all participants must stay on their knees.

Jump or Dive

This old camp pool favorite requires mid-air decision making. One at a time the young people take a nice, high bounce off the diving board. At the height of their jump, you yell either "Jump!" or "Dive!"—and the young person must obey. You'll see some wild contortions as kids try to change their water-entry positions in a split second. If a hand hits the water first, it's ruled a dive; if a foot hits first, a jump.

If the kids get too good at second guessing you, wait longer before you yell your command. Or really tie them in knots with an occasional "Jive!"

Laser Squirt

To get the same effect produced by expensive laser-tag guns, try this version of tag. Use water color marker to color a three-inch circle on a 4 x 6 card for each participant. Ask kids to bring their squirt guns and wear old shirts; you provide the buckets for refilling. Tape a card to the chest of each player—and have at it! When the colored circle is hit with water, the color runs—and that player is dead and out of the game.

Form five-person color-coded teams and allow a few minutes of pregame planning before signaling hostilities to commence. The team with the most unsquirted members at the end of the time period wins.

Missile Mania

Divide into two teams. The object of the game is to knock out the opposing team's launching pad. A launching pad is an area where designated players use giant slingshot water balloon launchers (available at many toy, novelty, or sporting-goods stores) to launch balloons over the open combat zone (OCZ) to hit any of the designated players inside the opposition's launching pad. (These designated players are the only ones who must remain inside their launching pad at all times.) Once a

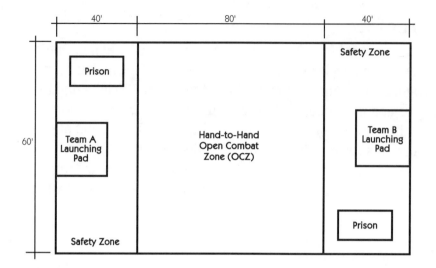

designated player is hit by a balloon, the pad is considered "knocked out" and the team scores a point.

Other players engage in hand-to-hand balloon combat in the OCZ as they try to knock out a launching pad by throwing the balloons. They also try to take opposition players prisoner by hitting them in the OCZ. (Those hit in the OCZ must remain in the opposition's prison until a knock out point is scored by their team, at which time they are freed and can return to the game.)

The safety zones are provided so a team's players can be immune from being taken prisoner. It is also off limits to the opposition's entrance unless they are being taken prisoner.

The team that scores ten knock out points first wins.

Pistol Pong

After a few matches of regular Ping-Pong, clear the table and give a pair of kids squirt guns. Place a Ping-Pong ball in the center; the dueling players, armed with the guns, should try to squirt the ball off their opponent's end of the table. Balls that fall off the sides of the table are replaced from where they fell, and play is resumed.

Variations? Try playing doubles, or set four players against each other on each side of a square table.

And be prepared for the inevitable fluid free-for-all finale.

Run 'n' Wet

Got your swimsuits on? Have your kids sit in a circle and number themselves off, then put a plump water balloon in the center of the circle. When the leader calls out two numbers, those two kids must jump up and run around the circle back to their own place—but no stopping yet. They must race through the empty spot they left to the water balloon in the middle.

Can you guess the rest? Yup—first one there gets to throw the balloon at the loser, who must stand still and not dodge it.

Save Queen Bertha

Here's a water-balloon strategy game for outdoors. Set up a battlefield (see diagram on next page) and provide each team with an equal number of three kinds of balloons:

• **Red** balloons (or another specified color) are worth 100 points.

• **Queen Bertha** balloons are very large (purchase at party-supply shops) and are worth 1,000 points. Only one per team.

• **A variety of smaller balloons** have no point value, but are weapons.

Teams begin the game in their own territory, attempting to advance their point water balloons beyond enemy territory and score them into the garbage can. Weapon balloons are thrown at carriers of point balloons; those carrying point balloons who get wet from an enemy's toss must relinquish their pointers to the enemy. This is the only way to steal points from the enemy—no physical contact is permitted, and no raiding enemy supplies.

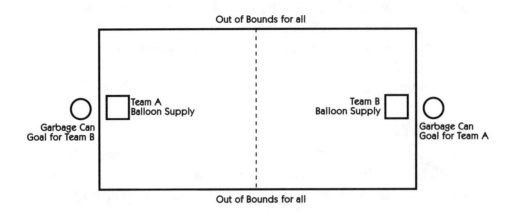

Out of Bounds for all

Garbage Can
Goal for Team B

Team A
Balloon Supply

Team B
Balloon Supply

Garbage Can
Goal for Team A

Out of Bounds for all

When about half the balloons are used, call a halftime so teams can re-evaluate their strategies. When all the balloons are gone, the team with the most points in its garbage can wins.

Search and Destroy

On the last day of camp, kids need an outdoor free-for-all, and—if you've been keeping track of team points all week—you need a final contest in which even the last-place team could conceivably catch up and win the entire week's competition.

So here's a combination scavenger hunt/water-balloon fight. First hide water balloons throughout the playing area (the more colors of balloons, the better). Begin the game by dividing players into teams and telling the rules:

• After players find balloons, they must run, crawl, walk, sneak, or bluff their way back to "headquarters," where a sponsor tallies the balloons and records the scores for the appropriate teams.

• Here's the twist: the point values of different balloon colors are not told to the players until the end of the game. (For example, yellow ones are twenty points each; blue, fifteen points; red, five points; white, minus five points, pink, minus ten points; three orange brought in on one trip by a player, thirty points.)

    • After the sponsor records players' points, the players are free to dispose of the balloons any way they want—and here's where the water-balloon fight begins.

    • Players continue the process of finding, recording, and destroying until time runs out.

To keep the scorekeeper's skin dry, deduct big points for lobbing balloons at them. And when the melee is over, conduct a brief but crucial game to see which team can pick up the most balloon pieces.

Slip and Slide Relay

For this exciting summertime game, use a commercial Slip 'N' Slide, or create a homemade one out of a heavy plastic sheet. Divide into teams and give each team member a cottage cheese container full of water. Players then run one at a time and slide on the wet surface, holding the cottage cheese container full of water with one hand over their heads. After sliding, the water from the cottage cheese container is poured into a bucket at the end of the plastic sheet. The team that can get the most water in its bucket within a given time limit is the winner.

Soaker

A hot outdoor afternoon is perfect for this water-balloon game. One person throws a water balloon high in the air and calls out another player's name (or number, if the group has numbered off). The player so called must catch the balloon. If the player succeeds at catching it unbroken, she gets a free shot at the thrower who called her name and gets her turn at throwing a water balloon up and calling another's name.

If the water balloon breaks during an attempt to catch it—well, that player gets soaked. And if a called-out player doesn't even attempt to catch it, turn the hose on him!

Soakin' Summer Softball

Make your softball (or Wiffle Ball or kickball) games into summer cool-offs with these wet versions.

- Lay a "wet banana," or Slip 'N' Slide, between third base and home and require runners to literally slide home all the way from third base.

- Substitute a lawn sprinkler for the bag at first base. Runners who hit a modest single must straddle the sprinkler. The more fortunate, who hit at least a double, have only to jump over the sprinkler on their way to second. A base runner on first and a pitcher with a slow windup equals one sopping player!

To keep both games moving, limit the batter to one pitch—either a hit or an out.

Sponge Dodge

In the heat of the summer, find a beach or open lawn, take along four or five five-gallon buckets and an equal number of sponges, and cool yourselves off with this game.

Mark out a circle somehow and place the buckets around the perimeter. Half fill them with water, and drop a sponge or two in each. After the entire youth group gets in the circle, the leader soaks the first sponge and throws. Those who get hit join the leader around the edge, and the game continues until only one is left—the winner. Sponges that drop inside the circle can be retrieved by any thrower, but they must be dipped again before they are thrown.

Some variations:

- Reverse the game. That is, when someone is hit, the thrower joins those inside the circle. Last one on the perimeter loses.

- Play by teams. Time how long it takes for one team to get all members of an opposing team hit and out of the circle. Shortest time wins. Or set a time limit—the winning team has the most members still in the circle when the clock runs out.

- Run the game indefinitely, with no winners or losers. Begin the game with five inside the circle. Whoever makes a hit trades places with the victim.

Taxi

This swimming pool game begins with two teams, each with an air mattress, on opposite sides of the pool. On "go" one member of each team straddles his or her mattress and paddles it around the pool. When the two arrive back at their own starting points, they each pick up another teammate and make another lap—and this continues until the entire team is on the mattress.

The trick is mounting the mattress, especially with several kids already on it. There'll be a lot of thrashing and sputtering during this game!

Ultimate Water Balloons

Remember *Ultimate Frisbee Football* (page 35)? Played with a Frisbee, that game combines teamwork with athletic prowess as the Frisbee is moved down the field in nonstop, continuous play with any one of a number of various twists to the game.

A favorite warm-weather variation is to substitute water balloons for the Frisbee. The referee should be supplied in advance with thirty-six filled water balloons (for an approximately thirty-minute game). These are stored up and down along the sidelines (allowing for quick replacement of the two balloons that the ref always carries in her or his hands). The referee must hustle to get a balloon to the other team when one breaks so the play is not unduly interrupted.

Water Baggies

The water balloon is an indispensable ingredient in youth ministry games. But how many hours do youth leaders spend filling balloons for the group?

One alternative is to have buckets of water ready and supply plastic sandwich bags, of the fold-lock top variety. As the game gets underway, the participants fill the bags by holding them under water and closing the top. The result is an instant, very temporary, water balloon substitute. Another advantage is that cleanup is easier than with regular water balloons.

Water-Balloon Soccer

On the next hot day when you're outside, divide the group into as many teams of ten to fifteen as you can. Before the game fill a minimum of three water balloons per team member. Also prepare one hat (or helmet) per team: with duct tape, affix tacks, point out, to a helmet or ball cap. The hat is then placed on an X on the ground about twenty feet from the starting line.

On a signal, the first person in line for each team runs to the hat and puts it on. The second person in the line lobs a balloon in the air in the general direction of the first player, who attempts to break the balloon with the hat. If the hat-wearing teammate misses, a second and third balloon are thrown. If he still doesn't puncture a balloon with his hat (and drench himself in the process), he puts the hat down and goes to the end of his line—and the next teammate in line tries her luck. The first team that cycles the entire team through wins the event.

Waterball Samurai

The object of this wet warfare is to hit the other team's samurai with a water-soaked foam ball as many times as possible in one minute.

Materials needed: Wiffle bat, foam balls (at least six), water buckets (at least three), step stool (from the water fountain), time keeper and point counter, chalk or tape.

Make boundaries for the game by drawing or marking with tape a six-foot-diameter circle. Place the low stool in the center of the circle. Fifteen feet outside the circle's edge, place three buckets on a line.

Divide the groups into teams of five or six players each, and ask each team to select one player to be the samurai. The samurai from the defending team stands on the stool in the center of the circle and may not step off the stool during the round. The remaining defending-team members position themselves on the perimeter of the circle to defend their samurai from the water balls. They can move neither into the circle nor beyond its perimeter. They must confine their movements to the edge of the circle. Their samurai, meanwhile, defends himself with a Wiffle bat to divert water balloons.

From behind the water-bucket line, the opposing team throws water-soaked foam balls at the samurai in the circle, attempting to hit him. If a thrown ball falls short of the circle, an offensive team member may run up to retrieve it and either carry it back to the line to throw it again or else toss it to one of the other team members already behind the line, who may then throw the ball at the samurai. Offensive players may not, however, enter the defending team's circle to retrieve any balls.

The round ends when one minute is up or all the water balls are inside the circle. The offensive team gets one point each time they hit the samurai with a water ball, or for each time the samurai steps off the step stool.

If you have more than three or four teams, you may want to get more foam balls and mark out more water-ball courts so you can have several games going on simultaneously. Winners from each court can play one another in a championship game.

Water Joust

This is an active game to be played in the shallow end of a swimming pool or lake. Equipment includes two large truck or tractor inner tubes, two boards (large enough to cover the inner tubes), two plungers, and two six-foot long broom handles.

Tie the boards onto the inner tubes and replace the plunger handles with the broom handles. Now you are ready to joust.

Divide your group into two teams. You will have four people (two from each team) in the water at a time. Each team will have one person in the water to maneuver the inner tube, while the other member is on the inner tube on his or her knees with the lance (broom stick with plunger) in hand. The object is to knock the other team's jouster off her or his inner tube.

Safety rules must be followed with this game! No swinging of poles or hitting is allowed—only straight-push "jousting." Have several sponsors positioned around the pool as monitors, and enforce the safety rules strictly.

Water Wars

Water Wars is similar to Capture the Flag, but not nearly as dry! Divide your participants into two teams. Each team has its own territory, set up as shown in the diagram with the following features:

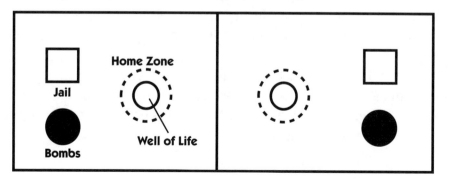

1. A large plastic garbage can filled with water. This is the "well of life."

2. A large plastic garbage can filled with 300 to 350 water balloons. The balloons are "bombs."

3. A bucket to throw well of life water on teammates and captives.

4. A jail to hold prisoners. This is a square area marked with chalk, large enough for several players to stand inside.

5. A source of water for each team to refill their well of life.

6. A home zone. This is a chalk circle marked around the well of life.

The object of the game is to tip over the other team's well of life. To accomplish this goal, each team has at least 300 water balloons. They go fast, so the more water balloons, the longer and better the game will be.

Players may enter enemy territory to attack opponents only when armed with a bomb. If opponents are hit with a bomb in their own territory, they are declared "dead" until someone from their own team throws a bucket of water on them from their own well of life.

If players are hit in enemy territory, they are taken prisoner and put in jail. The only way to escape jail is for a teammate to bring a bucket of water from his or her own well of life all the way across enemy territory, and throw it on the prisoner(s). In order for all players in jail to be released, they must be holding hands, or else all of them must get wet.

A player may not tip over the opposing team's well of life while armed. The home zone may not be guarded from within the white line. If an attacking player is hit with water before tipping the well of life, he or she becomes a prisoner and must go to jail. If a player moves successfully through enemy territory without getting wet and tips the opposing team's well of life over, his or her team wins. This game can go very quickly, so it's best played in a series of five or seven games.

CHAPTER 8

VOLLEYBALL GAMES

Black-Light Volleyball

If you can black out your gym and obtain four black lights, your kids will love this game of guesswork and strategy. With orange or green florescent spray paint, spray a volleyball, the top of the volleyball net, and—if they wear old shoes—your kids' shoes. Cut up old white towels or sheets for headbands, and have the kids bring either white gloves or gloves you can spray-paint. Get people to hold the black lights instead of merely standing the lights up around the volleyball court. This way the holder can dodge a wild ball and lights won't be broken.

Then turn off the white lights, turn on the black lights, and play volleyball! Since headbands, shoes, and gloves are the only clues to players' positions, the teams will scheme some strategy quickly—like slipping off their shoes in order to make a spike or momentarily hiding their heads and hands to outfox their opposition.

Double-Vision Volleyball

Play this volleyball game with two balls! After both teams serve their balls simultaneously on the ref's command, each ball is played until it scores a point for one of the teams. This means that either team can score with either ball, regardless of who served what ball. It also means that a team can score two points in a single, two-ball volley.

To compensate for the power plays of stronger players, use grocery-store-type, softer children's balls instead of standard volleyballs.

Headbangers' Volleyball

This is played like regular volleyball, except that boys can use only their heads to hit the ball. (If your girls feel slighted by the supposed sexism in this game, just tell them that the boys need a hit on the head to get their brains going.) The rules are as follows:

- Boys can use only their heads to hit the ball.

- Girls can hit the ball according to standard volleyball rules.
- A boy must hit the ball at least once every time the ball comes over the net, or that team loses a point.
- Each team can hit the ball five times to get it over.
- The ball can bounce once each time it comes over.

Otherwise, the game is played by the normal volleyball rules. This game is as much fun to watch as it is to play.

Human-Net Volleyball

This volleyball game uses not only the usual two teams, but a human net! Use a light, large ball (a beach ball works great) and divide into three teams; the third team becomes the net. Mark or tape a two-foot wide strip within which the net must remain; the other two teams may not enter the net's strip.

A regular volleyball game is then played—with the exception that the net plays, too, earning points for each ball it can catch as the other two teams attempt to play over the net. If the net merely knocks the ball out of play without catching it, no one scores. After each game, teams rotate either to the other side or into or out of the net strip.

You'll find that the net is often the strongest player!

Lottery Volleyball

This off-beat brand of volleyball adds a special element—the thrill of the unexpected. Divide into teams and position players as in conventional volleyball. The referee should stand a few feet out-of-bounds near mid-court with a container of "lottery tickets" numbered one through nine (have several of each number, and mix them up so that they can be drawn at random).

As the server serves, the referee draws out a ticket and calls out the number. The team receiving the ball must hit the ball that number of times (no more, no less) before returning it over the net. If they are successful, the serving team must do the same. Play continues requiring the same number of hits per play until a team fails. On the serve of the next round, a second ticket is drawn out and read, and play continues as before according to the number of hits required by the new ticket. Excitement will build on each play as team members count out hits, and you'll especially enjoy the groans when the referee calls out the dreaded number one.

All other conventional volleyball rules prevail, but you might want to liven things up by using water balloons instead of a ball, or by playing flamingo style (on one leg).

Mega Volleyball

Here's how to play volleyball with an extra-large group (twenty-four players or more at a time). You need three volleyball nets, four standard poles, string or line (tape for indoors) to mark the boundaries, two volleyballs, and a referee.

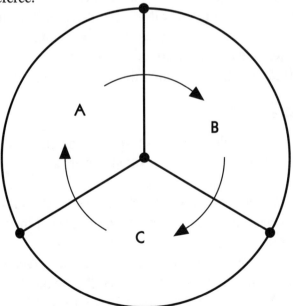

Place one pole in the center and the other three around it, so that the nets are stretched out from the center like spokes in a wheel (see the diagram). Make the boundary a circle so that each segment of the court is shaped like a pie slice (The three sections should be equal.)

Play is similar to regular volleyball, except that the ball is not returned across the net to the serving team. Instead, it advances to the third team, who sends it on to the first team, thus moving either clockwise or counterclockwise around the circle. In the diagram shown, A serves to B, who volleys to C, who must get the ball back to A, and so on. To keep the game fun, don't allow spikes. For added excitement, get two balls going at once!

As in a regular game, errors include misses, out-of-bounds volley, more than three contacts with the ball by the same team before it crosses the net, and more than one contact with the ball in immediate succession by the same player. Scoring, however, is different from regular play in that twenty-five points are given for every error. Thus the team with the lowest score wins.

Team Volleybasket

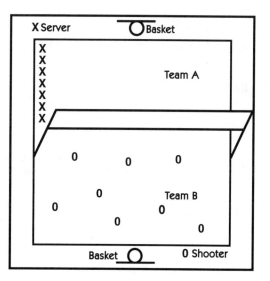

Divide the group into two teams on opposite sides of a volleyball net that is set in a basketball court. The serving team lines up along the sideline facing the server (see diagram), who does a normal volleyball serve from the normal serving position. After serving the ball, the server runs to the first person in line and gives that player a high five. That player in turn gives a low five to the next person, who gives a high five to the next, and so on to the end of the line. That last person then runs to the first person in the line and starts the process all over. Each time they complete the line (called the "slap-happy wave") they get one point.

Meanwhile, on the other side of the net, the volleyball is volleyed among the team members until it gets to the stationary shooter. It doesn't matter if the ball hits the ground during the volley. Players just pick it up and continue to volley to the shooter, who grabs the volleyball and shoots it, basketball-like, through the hoop. The shooter keeps at it until a basket is made, which also stops the action on the serving side of the net.

At that point the volleying team lines up facing the former shooter, who is now the server. The server makes a legal volleyball serve and starts the "slap-happy wave" while the receiving team volleys the ball back to its shooter. The serve alternates each time after the basket is made.

There are no points given for the basket—only for completing a slap-happy wave. The first team to twenty-one points wins.

Volleybowl

This fast-paced game is exciting for all ages, but especially for younger kids. You need two volleyballs, two bowling pins, and a large playing area (indoors or out).

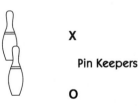

Team A X X X X X X X X X X X X

Team B O O O O O O O O O O O

Pin Keepers

X

O

Divide into two teams of equal size and have each team choose a "pin keeper." Then have each team line up, all members facing the same direction, in two parallel lines about fifteen feet apart. Set up a pin about ten feet in front of the first person in each line, and have the pin keepers stand behind their team's pin. Then give a volleyball to the first person in each line.

When a signal is given, the first players in each line attempt to knock down their team's pin, either by rolling or throwing the ball at it. If the pin is knocked down, the team gets a point. Then the pin keeper must set the pin up again and return the ball to the next person in line for play. If the pin is missed, no point is earned, and the pin keeper must return the ball to the next player in line. After each attempt, the player goes to the end of the line. Team members keep rotating in this way as fast as possible until the predetermined period of play (usually five minutes) is up. The team with the most points wins.

The excitement of the game is heightened if team members shout out their score after every successful attempt and when the two-minute and one-minute warnings are given. To add a wrinkle, use half-inflated balls or two balls for each team (a headache for the pin keepers); or have players stand with their backs to the pins and throw the ball between their legs while bending over forward.

Volley Feetball

This volleyball variation will keep your group light-footed. You play it according to most of the traditional volleyball rules, except for one big difference—the net is lowered to within a foot or two of the floor, and players can use only their feet to kick the ball under the net.

• Regular rules about out-of-bounds, team rotation, three-kick-per-team minimum, and such apply.

• During the serve, the players on both teams stand aside in order to let the serve reach the opposite team's back row—by traveling under the net, remember. After a back-row player has kicked the ball, players on both teams may move back into position and resume regular play.

- If a player in the front rows of the serving team touches a served ball before it goes under the net, it's side-out; if players in the front lines of the receiving team touch the ball before it reaches their team's back row, the serving team scores a point.

- If the back row of the receiving team lets a served ball go out-of-bounds untouched, the serving team scores a point.

- When a player kicks the ball over the net, of course, side-out or a point goes to the opposing team.

- Games are played to seven, fifteen, or twenty-one, depending on how much time you have.

Your kids will find the game a little tricky at first—they'll need to use the sides of their feet to kick with, soccer style. And you can always retreat to a smaller room with a Nerf ball and masking-tape boundaries.

Volleyslam

This baseball-like game played on a volleyball court requires two teams and any number of players. Home plate is under one of the baskets, and six bases are placed in the court's corners (see diagram on next page). The defensive team scatters itself throughout the gym. The batter stands at home plate and "bats" the volleyball with a normal underhand or overhand volleyball serve toward the far end of the court.

- Outs are made only by hitting runners with a thrown ball when they're between bases or when a "batted" ball hits the net—not by catching flies.

- A base may hold any number of runners, and runners may pass each other. A home run is scored if a "batted" ball hits the backboard, rim, or net at the opposite end of the court. (Invent your own award if the ball goes into the basket—for the feat certainly deserves one!)

- Since there's no catcher, a thrown ball that crosses the homebase

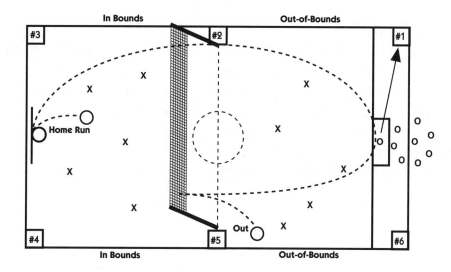

line is out of play. When the ball is out of play, runners must remain at the bases closest to them. Also notice that on the home-run side of the net, the area beyond the sidelines is still in-bounds.

• All team members bat once and only once in each inning—outs retire base runners instead of determining inning length.

• Points are awarded when runners reach sixth base or by home runs. The team with the most points after a designated number of innings wins.

Volloony Ball

On a basketball or volleyball court and across a volleyball net from each other, two opposing teams play a volleyball game—but with a weather balloon (or its equivalent). Since getting control of the balloon is a ticklish matter, a team gets up to (but not more than) ten hits before the balloon must be returned over the net. Similar to regular volleyball, a team earns points when their opponents (1) hit the balloon more than ten times, (2) allow the ball to touch the floor, (3) cause the ball to hit the ceiling or lights, or (4) hit the ball out-of-bounds.

Volloony Ball II

Here's an indoor volleyball game with a balloon—but to make the balloon heavier, faster, and more erratic, while keeping it soft, wrap it with three lengths of masking tape z. For a net, line up chairs or run a taut string between two chairs. All players play on their knees. Keeping score is optional—the kids will have a great time just making desperate saves and keeping the "ball" in the air. Have a few extra balloons on hand, for fingernails and double spikes that sandwich the balloon and tend to pop it.

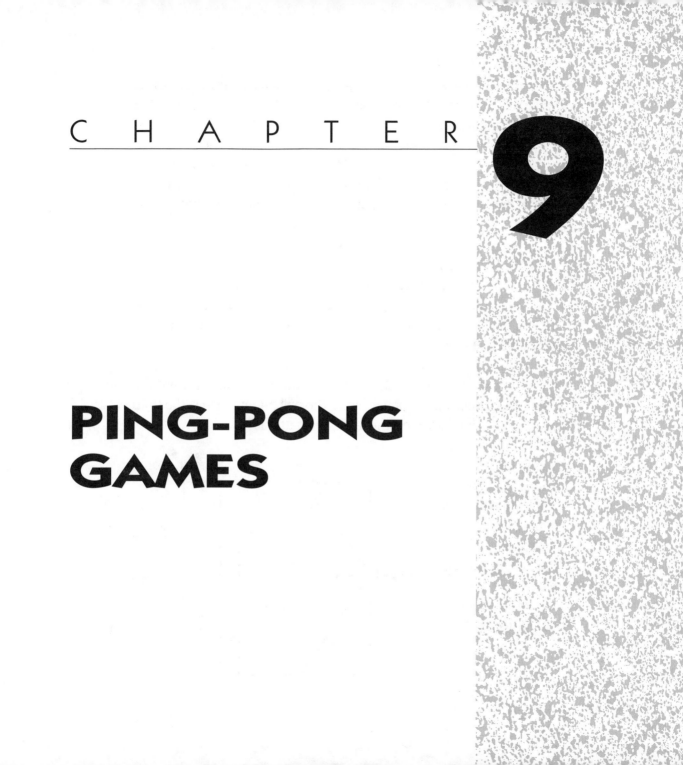

C H A P T E R

9

PING-PONG
GAMES

Baseball Ping-Pong

Using masking tape, mark off lines on a card table according to the diagram pictured below. You need foul lines and lines that indicate a base hit, a double, and a triple.

To play, place a Ping-Pong ball on home plate. The team "at bat" rotates one by one, attempting to blow the ball across the bases to a home run. The team "in the field" places on the opposite side of the table three players on their knees who attempt to blow the ball off the table before it scores a base hit.

Here are some additional rules:

1. The batter may blow only once.

2. The fielders may not touch the table at any time.

3. If the ball crosses the foul lines, the player at bat is allowed another blow, even if it was the fielding team that blew the ball back across the foul lines.

4. A ball's score is calculated at the point where it makes its farthest forward progress before being blown off the table toward the foul lines. For example, if the batter blows the ball and it reaches the third base tape before being blown off the table, the batter is credited with a triple. The next batter may get a double, putting two people on base—one on second, and the previous batter on third. The next batter may hit a home run, which would score three runs.

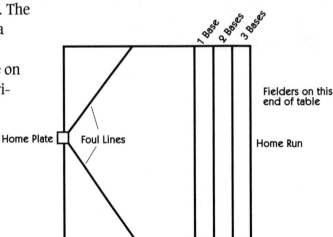

5. Outs are made by blowing the ball off the table before it reaches the first base line in such a way that it doesn't go back across the foul line.

6. Home runs are made by blowing the ball off the table on the opposite end from home plate. Fielders need to be careful about where they're blowing the ball; they can unintentionally score for the opposing team.

King Pong

If you have ever felt that the Ping-Pong table was just too short for your style of play, then this game could revitalize Ping-Pong for your group. Set two Ping-Pong tables end to end, and place the net in the middle. Play regular rules or invent twists like relay-round-robin, multiple hits per side, or teams of four or more. The results are as fun to watch as the game is to play.

Ping Pool

For a full hour of fun, try this Ping-Pong/pool-table hybrid. First, borrow one of those six-foot-long fold-up tables from the church kitchen or fellowship hall. Next, attach six Styrofoam cups along the edge of the table, one at each corner and one in the middle of each of the long sides—exactly like a pool table (see diagram below). Each cup should have its

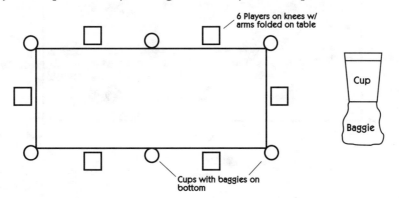

6 Players on knees w/ arms folded on table

Cup

Baggie

Cups with baggies on bottom

bottom punched out and replaced with a plastic Baggie, and the cups may need part of their top edges cut back and shaped in order to fit snugly to the table.

Now choose two teams of six players each and position them per the diagram—on their knees, with their arms folded along the edge of the table, and with their chins resting on their folded arms. Place on the table twelve Ping-Pong balls—six white ones for one team, six red ones for the other. (Use permanent marker to color the red ones so the color won't wear off during the game.) At the whistle, each team tries to blow its balls into the table's pockets. The players' arms will keep the balls on the table. A couple of helpers can put balls back into play that hop the barricade of arms.

But be careful—only two balls are permitted in any pocket. A referee makes sure this rule is followed during play. The team that sinks its balls first wins.

To vary the game, try some of these ideas:

Bumper Ping: Place unopened, ice-cold cans of soda on the playing table (see diagram below). Players must blow balls around the cans of pop to sink their balls in the pockets. The winning team gets the pop!

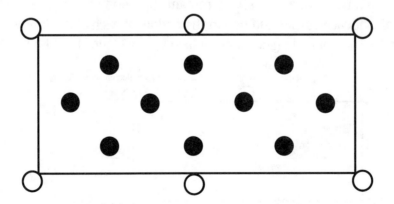

Tag-Team Ping: Only one member from each of two competing teams plays at the same time. When a person has successfully pocketed one ball, he tags a team member (those waiting for their turns sit apart from the playing table), who then represents the team at the table. The game is over when a team has pocketed all six of its balls, one ball per person.

Challenge Ping: Regular Ping Pool—except that only one ball of each color may roll into each cup.

Ping-Pong Blow

Players in this game spread themselves evenly around the edge of a large sheet, grab its edge, pull it taut (keeping it level), then attempt to blow a Ping-Pong ball off it. The players between whom the ball drops off the sheet are out, and the circle of players is gradually reduced.

Instead of a Ping-Pong ball, a balloon with a marble inside rolls around the sheet less predictably and so makes a challenging variation.

Ping-Pong Home-Run Derby

You can play this all-or-nothing version of baseball with just a handful of kids, a fair-sized room, a Ping-Pong ball, and a paddle (the "bat"). Set four or five folding tables on their sides as a playing field fence. Use masking tape to form a home plate and two foul lines.

Now for the rules:

• All players must play on their knees.

• There are no strikes, no balls, no base hits—just home runs or outs. The batting team tries to hit home runs—any Ping-Pong ball that clears the fence without touching the floor or ceiling scores as a home run. If a hit ball touches the floor or ceiling or is caught or swatted down by a fielder, the batter is out. Foul balls are played over.

• The fielding team, which plays along the inside of the fence, tries

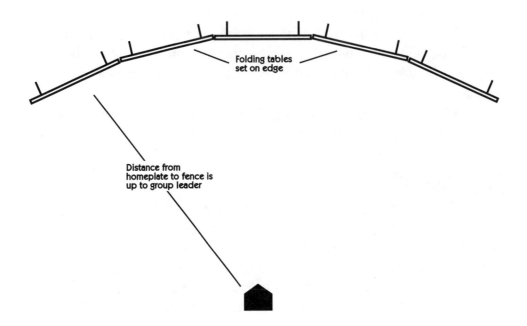

Folding tables
set on edge

Distance from
homeplate to fence is
up to group leader

to swat a hit at the Ping-Pong ball before it flies over the fence.

• Each team gets three outs; play as many innings as you like. The pitcher can be a sponsor who pitches to both teams or a member of the fielding team. You may choose to have an umpire and scorekeeper.

Ping-Pong Polo

Have team members make their own "polo sticks" by rolling up lengthwise several sheets of newspaper and using masking tape to secure the edges. The object of the game is for team members to knock the Ping-Pong ball into their team's goal using the polo stick. (Stockpile a few extra Ping-Pong balls to replace smashed balls.)

Set up goals by laying two tables on their sides (one table per goal), with the top of the table facing into the playing area. When the ball hits the face of the table, it will make a popping noise, indicating that a goal was scored. Each team should have one goalie who will guard the table. Goalies may use any part of their bodies to protect the table.

To make the game even more like real polo, have the kids ride broomsticks like horses while they play.

Ping-Pong Soccer

Play this game with as few as six people or as many as sixteen in a small gym or multi-purpose room. Use soccer rules, except there is no out-of-bounds, the goals are a lot smaller (hockey-sized), and players use a Ping-Pong ball instead of a soccer ball.

The game plays amazingly like soccer, largely due to the fact that a well-kicked Ping-Pong ball travels only fifteen to twenty feet. Have plenty of extra Ping-Pong balls, as they tend to get stepped on or squashed on a blocked shot. Penalize the team that breaks a ball by awarding the opposing team a free kick at the goal. This game can also be played using Ping-Pong paddles rather than kicks to pass the balls.

Power Pong

After clearing a room of all breakables, set up a Ping-Pong table and put out at least four paddles. Start the Ping-Pong game with two (or up to six) to a team. Serve and score according to standard Ping-Pong rules. Neither players nor their paddles can cross the plane of the net.

Now for the power—

• As in volleyball, each side is permitted as many as three hits before returning the ball across the net. A player cannot hit the ball twice consecutively.

• Walls, ceilings, and bodies are all in play.

• The ball is dead, and the point goes to the opposition, if the ball touches the floor.

Like volleyball, the key to winning is teamwork—accurate sets, smashing returns. Better have a few extra balls for this one.

Wall Baseball

During lock-ins, retreats, or any other indoor events, "Wall Baseball" is safe, fun, and doesn't require typical baseball skills in order for kids of any age to have fun playing it. Here's what you'll need: a wall (preferably 15' by 10', though any size will do), as well as masking tape and labels to duplicate on your wall the diagram below. Lay a home plate several feet out from the prepared wall and place a pitching rubber between the wall and home plate.

Now to play. With his or her back to the wall, the pitcher tosses a Ping-Pong ball to the batter, who attempts to hit it back toward the wall using a Ping-Pong paddle. Where the ball hits the wall determines the play. If the ball hits the "single" area, for example, then the batter gets a single and may proceed to first base. (Bases are set up as in a regular baseball diamond, but the distance between them is shorter to suit the room size.) Defensive players position themselves wherever they think they can catch fly balls or prevent balls from hitting the game wall. Other rules:

- All players play on their knees at all times.
- Balls that hit the floor or ceiling before hitting the wall are ruled as outs.
- If a batted ball hits a base runner, both the runner and the batter are out.
- Base runners must be forced out, not tagged out.
- No fast pitching.

Choose a plate ump to call obvious strikes and to decide where on the wall the ball hit in the case of a dispute. Play as many innings as you want.

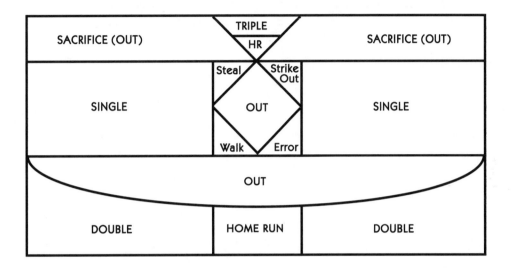

10

WIDE
GAMES

3-D Stratego

Here's a combination of Capture the Flag (*Play It!*) and Stratego, for which you'll need the standard Capture the Flag equipment—two flags and a big area with plenty of hiding places—as well as a couple decks of playing cards (or Rook cards).

After two teams are formed and they both have their flags, distribute to each player a playing card—a heart or diamond to red team members, and a spade or club to black teammates. The cards determine a player's rank—the king is the highest; then the queen; on down to the ace, who is lowest. The ace, however, is the only card that can beat a king.

Once play begins, both teams try to capture the opposing team's flag, according to normal Capture the Flag rules. When a tag occurs, both players reveal their cards. The highest-ranking card wins and continues playing, but the losing player goes to "Central Exchange"—someplace central in the game—in order to exchange his or her card for another (of the same color, of course). Only then can he or she rejoin the game. If both players in a tag have identical rank, both must go to the Central Exchange and exchange their cards for new ones. The winner is the first to capture the other's flag and return it to home territory.

For variety, you can make all number-ten cards "bombs," which can blow up all other cards. All number-five cards can form a "bomb squad," members of which are the only ones able to defeat the ten cards.

Mission Impossible II

This game is similar to Capture the Flag (*Play It!*)—it requires a large field, campgrounds, or woods. The object is for members of two teams to find their team's secret "M" bomb (watermelon) that was stolen and hidden by enemy agents (sponsors). In the process, players shoot each other with squirt guns filled with disappearing ink.

Scattered evenly through the playing area are six DMZs. Each of these demilitarized zones is about twenty-five feet in diameter (marked with flour or lime) and serves as an infirmary and ammunition depot. They're each equipped with a staff person, a pail of disappearing ink (read instructions, and dilute properly), and—at the beginning of the game—a third of a team's squirt guns.

Players should wear light-colored shirts in order for the disappearing ink to be seen; teams should be visually distinguishable—different colored squirt guns, arm bands.

The game begins this way: while students are gathered at HQ (a meeting hall or other central place) to receive their instructions, a staff member hides the two watermelons in the playing area. Rules the kids need to hear include these:

• The purpose is to find their team bomb and return it to HQ.

• When players are shot on their shirts, they are considered wounded and must go to the nearest DMZ and wait for the ink to disappear. The attending staff member then permits "recovered" players to rejoin the battle.

• While players are refilling their guns in the DMZs, they cannot be shot.

• "Recovering" players in the DMZ cannot refill their guns, but must wait until they are released and can go to another DMZ to refill.

• If a player finds the bomb but is shot as he's carrying it back to HQ, he must set it down gently (broken melons lose the game for the team that breaks them) and go to the DMZ as usual. Then either a teammate may pick up the bomb and attempt to finish the mission, or an opponent may take the bomb to hide it again.

After these rules are explained to the players, team members have five minutes to discuss their strategy. You may also want to have the initial squirt-gun filling done ahead of time by staff or by a few team members sent to the DMZs while the teams are laying battle plans. You'll probably need a whistle or bell to begin the game and then end it—perhaps after thirty minutes of playing if neither team has won by then.

Afterwards, enjoy the watermelons!

Murder Mystery

In this game the kids are detectives questioning suspects in an effort to find the killer of Mr. John Stone. The five suspects (Mr. Mun, janitor; Steve Stone, John's brother; Sam Swade, lawyer; Mrs. Stone, John's wife; and Ms. Wright, secretary) are prepared ahead of time to act their parts using the scripts provided (pp. 156-60). They should come costumed for their parts—the secretary looking seductive, the lawyer shady, the janitor in overalls, and so on. The players are divided into groups of five or six and will attempt to solve the mystery by working within their groups.

The game begins with everyone seeing the scene of the murder (see "Setting Up the Murder Scene" on page 155) and hearing the scripted opening comments given by the host. After the opening, each suspect leaves for a separate room, and the groups of detectives move from room to room questioning the suspects (one group in a room at a time, with a time limit of five or ten minutes per visit). Groups may visit any suspect as many times as they like.

At the conclusion of the game, all groups return to the scene of the murder and write on a piece of paper who they think killed John Stone and how and why they think the murder took place. The game leader then reads all the solutions offered by the kids as well as the solution provided (see "Solution to the Mystery" on pp. 161-62).

The success of this game lies with the actors playing the five suspects. Skillful youths may play these parts, but it usually works out better with adults. Before the game is played, the suspects meet to listen to each others' scripts and hear the solution to the mystery; for during the game itself the detectives will ask many questions not covered by the scripts, and although the suspects may say, "the question you asked is not relevant," suspects may also ad-lib on the story line as long as it does not conflict with or give away the solution. This can only be done if they already know each others' material.

Each suspect's script is divided into two parts: an alibi and a confession (the janitor has three parts). Suspects tell their alibi to every group, but they only offer their confession if the detectives can prove by quoting evidence from other suspects that the suspect being questioned is lying. For example, many suspects will claim that they were not at the office that night, but the janitor will place them all at the scene. When the detectives tell the suspects that the janitor testifies to seeing them at the office, the suspects spill their guts, giving the second parts of their scripts.

The suspects must use discretion in their answers. If they are stingy with information, the game will go on too long; if they too readily tell all, the detectives will catch on too quickly. The janitors first part is rather simple, but the key phrase is when he says that he found the body while checking to see if John and his friends had left. The janitor gives his second part only when the detectives ask if he saw others there.

Setting Up the Murder Scene

The scene is a business office containing a desk and a table (or bookshelf) holding an aquarium. The office is topsy-turvy from an apparent struggle. Papers and file folders are strewn about the room and on the desk. Clearly visible among the papers on the floor is a broken picture frame containing a photo of the actress who plays the part of Mrs. Stone. On the desk is an agenda showing meeting times as follows: secretary 8:00 p.m., Steve Stone 8:30 p.m., Sam Swade 9:15 p.m. The aquarium is tipped over with the gravel falling off the edge of the table. Add some broken glass around it, and on the floor beneath it place some dead fish (from a local pet store's casualties) or cutouts of fish. Also below the aquarium trace the outline of a person with either chalk or masking tape to indicate where the body was found. Add some ketchup, broken glass, and water around the outline of the head.

Opening Comments to Players

This is the office of John Stone, who was murdered last night. The janitor found him on the floor at 10:00 p.m. The cause of death was a blow to the back of his head, and the time was between 8:00 and 10:00 p.m. From the agenda on the desk, we know that he was working late and was to see his secretary at 8:00 p.m., his brother Steve Stone (who was his business partner) at 8:30 p.m., and his lawyer Sam Swade at 9:15 p.m. We have all three of these people here for you to question. We also have Mr. Stone's wife here, as well as the janitor who found the body.

Your job is to find out who killed John Stone and how and why they did it. That is, by evidence at the scene and from what you hear from the suspects, you must prove who the murderer is, the motive for the murder, and the method of the murder. Once you know this information, write it on a paper. We will read all your conclusions at (*insert the time you will conclude the game*), then I will tell you who is right.

Some suggestions: You are investigators. When you get some evidence, use it to get more information. One or more of these people will be lying, but if you confront suspects with evidence, they will come clean. For instance, if you find out that one of the suspects made a death threat, do not say to that person, "Did you say you would kill John Stone?" Say instead, "I have a witness who will testify that you said you were going to kill John Stone."

The suspects are working from a script and will not have answers to all your questions. If they seem to be making up answers to some of your questions, it is not always a clue that they are lying. They may be trying to give an appropriate answer that will not at the same time lead you off the track. They may also decline to answer, saying that your question is not relevant to the case.

Mrs. Stone, John's Wife

Alibi: All I know is my husband was a good man, and I don't know why anyone would want to kill him. I was home all night long until 10:00 p.m., when the police called and (*begins to cry*) told me John had been killed.

Confession: I had a phone call from someone. He would not give his name, but he said my husband was having an affair with his secretary. I had suspected it for a long time and had told several of my friends that if I found out it was true I would kill him. When I got the call I went to his office. I was very angry, but I was not going to kill him. When I got there, the place was a mess. Papers were everywhere, my picture was smashed, and the carpet was soaked from the broken aquarium. It looked like there had been a terrible fight. John was (*attempting to retain emotional control of herself*) lying there—blood all over the back of his head. I can still see him in my mind—his blank expression and all those fish wiggling.

Mr. Sam Swade, Lawyer

Alibi: I was scheduled to meet with John Stone at 9:15 to finalize the signing of some business papers that he and his brother were working on. But my paging service left a message with me that someone had called and canceled the appointment. She didn't say who called—I just assumed it was John. The message said the meeting would be rescheduled for the next day sometime, so I never went to John's office. The first thing I heard was when the police called me at home around 10:00.

Confession: Yes, I did go to John's office at 9:15. When I walked in, John was lying on the floor. Things were messed up—papers all over the floor, some pictures were broken. I went around to look at John close. There was a little blood on the floor, which seemed to come from the back of his head. I could tell by looking at him he was dead.

I was going to call the police, but first I had to check on some records. Steve Stone had been having some power struggles with his brother, and I had helped him falsify some records so he could gain more power in the company. When I looked, though, the records were gone. Steve was the only one who knew about them, so I knew he had to be the one who took them. I knew he was hungry for power. In fact, although I can't prove it, I think he was blackmailing John.

Two days before his death John told me somebody was blackmailing him. He had been having an affair with his secretary, Sandy Wright, and told me someone was getting him for big bucks to keep it from his wife. He asked me for advice on how to get out without legal problems. I told him the first step was to break the relationship with Ms. Wright and get her as far away from him as possible. In fact, he was going to do that when she brought the papers by the night of the murder. I'm innocent. I didn't kill John Stone. He was dead when I got there. The more I think about it, the more the finger points straight to Steve Stone.

Mr. Steve Stone, Brother to John

Alibi: I had a meeting set up with my brother to finalize some papers on an account we had been working on. I was to meet him at this office at 8:30, but I had an emergency come up and was not going to be able to make the meeting. I called several times to tell John I wasn't coming and that he should make whatever decisions had to be made and that I'd back whatever he thought was best, but I never got an answer at his office. I never left my office. In fact, I was still there when the police called to tell me John had been murdered.

Confession: Yes, I was at John's office at 8:30 for our meeting. When I walked in he was on the floor. There were signs of a struggle—some pictures were broken, some papers were scattered on the floor. I went to look at John, and there was a small pool of blood from a blow to the back of his head. I would have called the police, but my brother and I had been having some problems.

You see, John was greedy for power and money (*getting angry now*). He was trying to cut me out of the business. I had been working with our lawyer, Sam Swade, to steal the control of the company from John. There were some papers in John's office we had falsified, and I thought it would be best if I got them out of the office before I called the police. But I couldn't find them. That's when I knew Sam Swade must have killed John. He was a crook to begin with, and there's no telling what kind of deals he's been pulling. I didn't know what to do, so I left and went back to my office as if I'd never left there and waited until the police called.

I didn't kill him. He was already dead when I got there. I couldn't kill him. He was my brother! But I'd bet Sam Swade is behind this.

Mr. Mun, Janitor

Alibi: I had been working in the building like I always did. Mr. Stone told me he had a late meeting, which was not uncommon. So about 9:55 I went by to make sure he and his friends were gone before I locked up. When I walked in, it was a pitiful sight. Someone had torn the place to bits, and Mr. Stone was dead on the floor. As soon as I saw him, I called the police.

Confession A: (*Use this speech only if the detectives ask who you saw come in.*) Well, his secretary came by to drop off some papers. I was cleaning the hall. She went in and came right back out. Then a while later I saw Mr. Stone's brother going through the main lobby. I'm not sure how long he was there because I didn't see him leave. A little later I saw Mr. Stone's lawyer, Sam Swade, getting out of his car in the parking lot, but I didn't see him leave, either. Mrs. Stone must have also been there because her coat was on the rack when I went to lock up around 9:50. But it wasn't there when I had cleaned the hall at 8:00.

Confession B: Okay, I was cleaning the hall when Ms. Wright came by with the papers. She went into the office. After a little while I heard glass break and some yelling. I came down the hall and walked into the office. As I did I saw Mr. Stone coming around the desk toward Ms. Wright. As he got to her she pushed him away and he tripped and fell backwards. His head hit the aquarium and it busted everywhere. Then he fell to the floor. I checked him for his pulse, but he was dead.

I knew it was an accident, so I told Sandy—ah, Ms. Wright—to go home, that it was an accident, and that I would make it look like someone had robbed the place. She left, but before I could do anything, Mr. Stone's brother showed up. He saw his brother, then snooped around the place looking for something. He finally left. When I was sure he had gone, I started again to make the place look like a robbery. But then Mr. Swade came down the hall. He looked all over the room also, but didn't leave with anything. Not long after that Mr. Stone's wife came and then ran out. After that I just messed the place up a little and called the police. I was trying to help Ms. Wright.

Ms. Sandy Wright, Secretary

Alibi: I came by the office at 8:00 to drop off some papers for Mr. Stone. He needed them for some meetings he was having that evening. I was only there for a minute. He was on the phone, so I left them on his desk. He said thanks, and I left. That's all I knew until the police called me at my home around 10:00 to tell me Mr. Stone was dead.

Confession: Yes, I was having an affair with Mr. Stone. When I came in to drop off the papers, he told me it was all over—I was being let go Monday, and he told me not to ever set foot in the place again. He treated me like some undesirable business call. I was hurt and angry. I pulled his wife's pictures off the wall and broke them. Then I started yelling at him. He started toward me from around the desk. I didn't even want him to touch me, so I pushed him away and he tripped over the lamp cord and hit his head.

Then he just laid there and didn't move at all. I didn't mean to kill him. It was an accident (*starts crying*). You can ask the janitor. He heard the pictures breaking and heard the yelling and came into the office just as John fell and hit his head. He told me he knew it was an accident. He said for me to go home and he would make it look like a break-in and robbery. I did it because I looked so guilty and was afraid. I swear I did not mean to kill him.

Solution to Murder Mystery

John Stone was in his office at 8:00 when his secretary, Ms. Wright, (with whom he had been having an affair) came in. On the counsel of his lawyer, John broke off the relationship with her and let her go as his secretary to avoid being blackmailed. She reacted violently, smashing the picture of John's wife. John came around the desk to try to restrain her, but she pushed him away. He tripped, falling backwards and hitting his head on the aquarium stand. He fell unconscious on the floor, but not dead. The janitor came in just as John hit his head and fell to the floor. He saw it as an accident and told Ms. Wright to go home and he would make it look like a robbery.

Before he was able to do this, however, Steve Stone came in. Seeing the mess and his brother on the floor, he went to the file and took out some papers he had falsified so that he could steal the company from his brother. He felt that if they were found it would make him look guilty of killing John. He was sure that the lawyer had killed his brother and was going to pin it on him. He then went back to his office and waited there as if he had never left.

Again the janitor was unable to finish making the place look like a robbery because the lawyer came in. He also looked for the papers that Steve had taken. When he could not find them, he figured that Steve was the murderer and that he was going to use the papers to frame him. So he also left and created an alibi.

Soon after this John's wife received a call telling her that John was having an affair. When she came down she was out for blood, but it had already been shed. When she saw the mess, she was afraid that it would look like she had indeed killed her husband in a fit of rage. She also left, but what she saw was a main piece of evidence. She said that the fish were alive at 9:50, which meant that the aquarium could not have been broken by the secretary at 8:00. However, no one else had mentioned the aquarium being broken—except the janitor. Mr. Mun said Ms. Wright pushed John, and his head hit the aquarium, breaking it.

When Sam Swade left John's office, the janitor again tried to mess up the room. His intent was not simply to make it look like a robbery, but to really rob John Stone. Since he believed his blackmail scheme was already destroyed (Mr. Mun thought John was dead), he decided to remove the safe keys from John's body, clean the place out, and pin the murder and robbery on Ms. Wright, Steve Stone, or Sam Swade. But as he searched John's pockets for the keys, John began to wake up. Mr. Mun picked John up enough to strike his head again, this time truly killing John Stone.

To cover his tracks, he called John's wife and told her John was having an affair. He knew she suspected it and had overheard her threatening John in the office. He did not anticipate that it would be her testimony that would put him away.

Penetration

Have a large group, a large building with several entrances, and a dark night? Then you're set for "Penetration"!

The object is to "break" into the building, read a message that clues you in to the whereabouts of the treasure, find the treasure, and deliver it to a predetermined leader—all without being caught by guards and imprisoned.

First, divide any number of young people into two teams. Then choose your guards: they must be adult leaders or unbiased kids, for the guards must be absolutely neutral, arresting members of both teams impartially. They will patrol the building in pairs, clockwise—never counterclockwise—in order to catch players, arresting anyone they can shine their flashlights on directly. When this happens, the guard shouts, "Stop for identification!" The players so caught must stop immediately and allow themselves to be escorted to jail, where they must remain for ten minutes or until another player breaks them out.

A jailbreak is achieved when a player enters the jail, tags a prisoner, and then both of them flee—all without being detected by guards. What keeps this game active is this: a player earns 100 points for breaking anyone out of jail—even members of the opposing team. Like the guards, the jailer must be an impartial player who never alerts guards, but merely verifies that jailbreaks are legitimate, tallies points for both teams, and settles any disputes.

For more suspense, place a searchlight on the flat roof of the building, and rotate it slowly or turn it on for a few seconds every five minutes or so.

What "Penetration" requires is trust—common honesty. When a patrolman gets you in his beam, for example, you need to freeze for the game to continue enjoyably. You must similarly cooperate as you're escorted to jail. Games with trust factors teach kids the benefits of honesty and fair play—and are great discussion starters for later, too.

Where's Waldo?

Where, where, where, where's Waldo? Everywhere you go, people are looking for Waldo. Have you seen him? Rumor has it that he's in a mall near you. So instead of looking for pictures, this time your group will be looking for people.

To play this exciting version of Where's Waldo?, secure one person to dress like Waldo and ten others to carry or wear the following items that belong to Waldo: scroll, message in a bottle, flag, skates, deck of cards, bird's nest, a baseball bat, a football, a duck, and a cane.

As the leader of the game, you need to dress like Wizard Whitebeard, wearing a wizard's robe, hat, and of course a white beard. Have your volunteers get to the local mall or shopping center thirty minutes ahead of your group. When your group arrives, form teams of three to four players each, give each team a game sheet (see sample) and instruct them to meet at a designated location (like the ice cream store) as soon as they find Waldo and all of his items or when time expires (usually an hour)—whichever comes first.

Rules of the game:

1. Be kind, courteous, and polite at all times. In other words, don't be rude and obnoxious!

2. When approaching someone, ask "Are you Waldo?" or "Is that Waldo's (name a listed item)?"

3. The first team to find Waldo and all of his items (within the time limit) or the team with the most points (if no one team finds every item within the time limit) is the winner.

4. Instruct your group where to meet at the designated time.

5. When they find Waldo or his belongings, have the person with the item verify the find by signing his or her name on the game sheet.

6. Then Wizard Whitebeard told his Waldo watchers: "Continue on your journey and never rest until you have found Waldo and all of his personal items. For in finding them you will help Waldo understand the purpose of his journey; then he will see the truth about himself. Let the search begin!"

Where's Waldo?	
1. Waldo's scroll	7,000 pts.
2. Waldo's message in a bottle	8,000 pts.
3. Waldo's flag	2,000 pts.
4. Waldo's skates	3,000 pts.
5. Deck of cards	6,000 pts.
6. Waldo's duck	4,000 pts.
7. Waldo's bird nest	2,000 pts.
8. Waldo's baseball bat	2,000 pts.
9. Waldo's football player	5,000 pts.
10. Waldo's cane	8,000 pts.

11

MIXERS

Birthday Shuffle

Similar to Fruitbasket Upset (*Play It!*), everyone sits in chairs in a big circle for this game. One extra person stands in the middle of the circle, without a chair. The leader calls out any three months of the year, and everyone in the circle whose birthday is in one of those months must get up and find a new chair. While they're scrambling to find a new seat, the extra person tries to sit in a vacant chair, leaving a new player stuck in the middle.

If most of the kids in the group are roughly the same age, the leader can call out a year, and all those who were born that year must switch chairs. If the leader calls out some other predesignated word or phrase (like "Happy Birthday!"), then everyone must get up and change chairs.

Candy Quiz

Hand out the quiz on the next page as an individual challenge or a small-group project. Each phrase is a clue to the name of a candy bar.

ANSWERS

1. MUSKETEERS
2. TWIX
3. MOUNDS
4. MILKY WAY
5. RED HOTS
6. MARS
7. HOLLYWOOD
8. O'HENRY
9. SNICKERS
10. BUTTERFINGER
11. M & M'S
12. CLARK BAR
13. BABY RUTH
14. 5TH AVENUE
15. KISS
16. PAYDAY
17. SLOW POKE
18. BLACK COW
19. JUNIOR MINTS
20. MILK DUDS
21. BIT-O-HONEY
22. ALMOND JOY
23. REESE'S PIECES
24. SWEET TARTS
25. ROLOS

Quiz

1. A famous swashbuckling trio of old_____
2. Elmer Fudd's sleight of hand or magical maneuvers_____
3. Places of interring enemies of those who tend and drive cattle and who are usually mounted on domesticated, large, solid-hoofed, herbivorous mammals_____
4. A broad, luminous, irregular band of astral lights that encompasses the stellar sphere_____
5. Crimson-colored libidinous cravings_____
6. A celestial body fourth in order from the sun, conspicuous for the redness of its light; its planetary symbol is ♂_____
7. The hard fibrous xylem substance produced by the Aquifoliaceae family of shrubs and trees characterized by their thick, glossy, spiny-margined leaves and usually bright red berries_____
8. Author William Sidney Porter's pseudonym_____
9. Multiple expressions of mirth, joy, or scorn in a covert or suppressed manner_____
10. An idiom, used here singularly, employed to describe one whose dexterous deficiency denies proficiency in getting a grip on goods_____
11. Possessive clone alphabetical characters_____
12. A saloon named after the newspaper-reporter alias of a superhero_____
13. Childhood name of a former renowned baseball player whose strike-out record is recondite_____
14. Celebrated street in the Big Apple_____
15. Labial massage_____
16. The 24-hour part of the week set aside to compensate for labor or toil_____
17. A sluggish jab_____
18. Ebony-colored country critter_____
19. Subordinate herbs or seasonings_____
20. Lactic flops_____
21. A morsel of regurgitated sweet viscid material from the social and colonial hymenopterous insect_____
22. The jubilant sensation of an ellipsoidal and edible nut_____
23. Label on the body bag containing the remains collected after a cat named "Reese" was run over by a mower_____
24. Dissonant confectionery mixture of dulcet and piquant seasonings_____
25. To rotate several members of the cylindrical-shaped component of the vowel family_____

Connect-a-Name

This get-acquainted activity uses only a large piece of paper and a magic marker. Form teams of four to six people each. For round one, at a signal each team attempts to connect every team member's first name in one crossword puzzle (see diagram below) in the shortest amount of time. For round two combine two teams and play again. Continue playing rounds until all players are in one big team making a crossword puzzle of all the names. Display the final crossword during a Bible study on 1 Corinthians 12 to illustrate that all Christians are part of the same body.

```
KYLE
 E
EVA
 I    J
NELLIE
      L
     LANCE
```

Cross 'Em Up

Ask players to think of one thing about themselves that not everyone knows and write that on index cards that you hand out. Collect the cards and use the information to create clues to a group crossword puzzle, with the kids' first names as the answers in the puzzle. (Many computers have a crossword puzzle program that makes this project easier to complete.)

Across

1. Member of the drill team at school
3. Father is a United Airlines pilot
7. Heavyweight wrestling champion
8. Family owns A & B Market
10. Friend of Angi's from Piner High School
11. Plays the drums in a band
12. Tennis star at Piner
15. Duran Duran fan
19. Loves any sport
21. A track star and on student council
24. Our football hero
26. "The Motorcycle Kid"
28. "The Hick"
29. Just moved here from Texas
31. Has a last name like "Rock"
33. Esoteric (Don't try to figure this one out, just write the word.)
34. Loves to dance
35. Loves horses

Down

1. Likes board games
2. Just got braces
4. Likes to play tackle football
5. Favorite sport is tennis
6. Loves to run track
7. Loves marine biology
9. Favorite hobbies: swimming, dancing, boys
13. Plays basketball
14. Grew up in Florida
16. Was in the play *Grease* at school
17. Recently injured left hand
18. Wants to be a school teacher
20. Worked the light board at school plays
22. Drives a '66 Mustang
23. Drives a '67 Mustang
27. Has a dog names Amos
29. Dad sells life insurance
30. Loves to golf
32. Collects stickers

Dot to Dot

Before this game, buy two packages (each package a different color) of half-inch, self-sticking circle labels and number them one through half the number of kids in your group—that is, if there are thirty in your group, number one color of circles one through fifteen. Do the same for the other color circles. Bring along a couple balls of kite string or embroidery yarn as well as some rolls of masking tape.

Divide the kids into two teams (or more, if your group is large), give each team a package of the numbered circle labels, instruct all players to stick a circle on their foreheads—then have them mingle, perhaps playing another crowd breaker so that the members of the two or more teams are thoroughly mixed. At a signal all players stand still, and a selected captain from each team uses the string and tape to string together her or his team dot-to-dot fashion, in order according to the number stuck to the players' foreheads. Captains can tape the string wherever they want on their teammates, and the first team finished wins.

Can you guess the fitting reward? A children's dot-to-dot book!

Food, Glorious Food

Fit this game into your yearly banquet or one of your food events. It could also be played as part of the Planned Famine or other food/hunger aware-ness service project.

1. Find two other people born in your same group of months by making the appropriate sound for your food group.

Jan/Feb/Mar	--Bread	--"I've got the eaties for my Wheaties!"
Apr/May/Jun	--Meat	--"Oink, oink, oink!"
July/Aug/Sept	--Vegetables	-- Shout out your least favorite vegetable
Oct/Nov/Dec	--Dairy	--"Moo!"

2. Once you have formed your group of three, together name six edible objects that begin with the letter "S." Have one of the group initial here: _____

3. Find a partner from somewhere in the room and quickly shout together "Smorgasbords are disgusting!" seven times. Have your partner initial here: _____

4. Locate someone who likes liver and have him or her initial here: _____ (Gag!)

5. Grab a new partner and count each other's teeth. Write the number of teeth your partner has here: _____ and have him or her initial here:_____

6. Say to a new partner you don't know the "two all-beef patties, special sauce, lettuce, cheese, pickles, onions on a sesame seed bun" line three times.
Have that person initial here: _____

7. Get another partner and see if you can "pinch an inch." If you can, tell that person he or she should eat more Special K

8. Have someone lift you off the ground and guess your weight. If the person guesses too low, wink at him or her. If the person guesses too high—slap him or her.
Initial here: _____

Human Crossword

Make up a crossword puzzle similar to the one pictured with "limbs" that branch off at a variety of places in the puzzle. Plan your crossword so that several names of your young people will fit into the puzzle—but add some extra word-spaces that allow for player creativity. Award prizes to those who get the most names into their puzzles.

Instruct the students to find people whose names will fit into the puzzle in the allotted time. First, middle, or last names can be used. Letters must match up with adjoining names. Nicknames and abbreviations are allowed (Rodney/Rod, yes. Darren/Dar, no). To get you started, two "freebie" names are included (see next page).

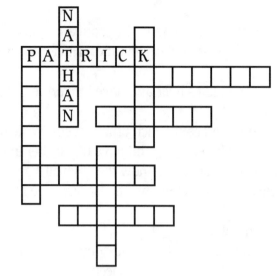

Staff 6/00

Mix 'Em Up

Set up a circle of chairs, one for each player except the leader. Have all the players sit.

The leader starts out by calling a random characteristic of players present (for example, everyone with purple socks). All players who fit the characteristic then move to seats vacated by other players doing the same thing. The leader also finds a seat. After all the seats have been taken, another player will be left standing. This player then does the same thing.

The player in the middle can also say, "Mix 'em up"; in response, all players must get up and find new seats.

Nose Names

Write celebrity names on individual file-folder labels. Players all stick a label on their noses so that they can read each others' labels, but not their own. Players try to guess the name of the celebrity on their noses by asking yes or no questions of other players.

Labels can also be stuck on the forehead, chin, cheeks.

6/00 Staff

Time Bomb Ice Breaker

The prop used in this mixer is a small, gift-wrapped box with a removabl cover and a travel alarm clock inside. On the cover these instructions appear:

"You have just been handed a time bomb. Hear it ticking? The only way you can get rid of it is to introduce yourself to a stranger in the room and tell that person where you're from; then find out that person's name and where he or she is from. After introductions, you may hand that person this gift."

The time you allow them, to make introductions before the alarm goes off will vary depending on the size of the crowd, but the average is about five minutes. You can use more than one bomb for a larger crowd. When the alarm goes off, whoever is caught with the bomb is marked with a Band-Aid on the forehead and seated in the middle of the room. "Victims" can be used later as "volunteers" for whichever activities may need them. They will also be the ones to set/reset the alarms for a shorter period of time during which the introductions continue. This gift exchange goes on until you have as many volunteers as you need for other events, or about fifteen minutes, depending on the size of the group.

Shuffle the Deck

Here's a simple, lively way to break a large group down into smaller ones—or to play just for fun. Distribute a deck of playing cards (or Rook cards) to the group, one per person. Then call out different combinations, like these:

- "Get in a group that adds up to fifty-eight."
- "Find three people of the same suit."
- "Find five numbers in a row, of any suit."
- "Find your whole suit."
- "Find four of you—four threes, four eights, and so on."

For larger groups use multiple decks of cards, for smaller groups eliminate cards. Create your own combinations.

QUIET
GAMES

Drawing in the Dark

In a dark room or with tightly closed eyes, participants must make a pencil drawing of a scene you describe to them.

Give every student a sheet of paper and a pencil. The idea is to direct them to draw portions of the entire picture in the dark so they can only guess at the accurate place to place an object. Turn out the lights, then tell them to draw, say, a house in the middle of the paper. Then ask them to place a tree to the left of the house. Then add a snowman to the right. Now put a chimney on the roof of the house. Draw a mailbox by the door. Draw a boy by the snowman. Put a scarf on the boy. Put smoke coming out of the chimney. Draw a dog by the tree. Put curtains in the window, and a hat on the snowman, a nest in the tree, a flag on the mailbox, and so on. Post the masterpieces at the end of the game.

Find the Mailman

Tell kids that it's April 15 and your tax forms need to get to the post office. Hold up a fat envelope and tell them you have the tax forms, but they have to figure out who the mailman is.

Ask everyone to sit in a circle. Give one player your envelope of tax forms and ask her to wait outside of the room. Now choose another person to be the mailman, and assign him a mannerism like one of these:

Blinks a lot
Answers questions by saying "Awesome!"
Sits with legs crossed
Arms are always folded
Taps his foot
Name is Mr. Mailman
Sleepy, yawns
Ends each sentence with "... you know?"
Scratches head a lot

Laughs a lot

Always says "I don't know"

Always asks if you need some stamps

Twiddles his thumbs

Licks his lips a lot

Can't talk

Shifts in his chair a lot

Puts his arm on his neighbor's chair

Smiles a lot

Ends each sentence with "Have a nice day!"

Hands have both index fingers pointing at you

Winks at you

Coughs a lot

Wears someone else's jacket

When the player holding the tax envelope (IT) enters, tell her she has a time limit (one to three minutes, depending on the size of your group) and a limit on how many questions she can ask each student in the circle—say, three questions per player—by which time she must put the envelope in the mailman's hand. Suggest to her that she pay attention to body language as well as peculiarities in how kids answer her questions. Players must respond honestly to ITs questions.

Four on a Couch

Write all players' names on individual slips of paper and place them in a hat. Four of the players sit on the "couch" (the couch can be four chairs next to each other), two boys and two girls (boy, girl, boy, girl alternating). The remaining players sit in a circle on the floor, leaving one open space in the circle. All players then draw a name from the hat.

The object of the game is to fill all four spaces on the couch with either all boys or all girls. The person sitting in the circle with the open space on his or her left starts by calling the name of one of the people in the group. Whoever is holding the slip of paper with that name on it moves to the open spot in the circle and trades slips of paper with the person who called the name. The person now sitting with the open spot on his or her left continues the play. The game ends when the couch has either all boys or all girls sitting on it.

Here's where strategy comes in. Sharp players will remember which players are holding whose names. When they have a turn to call a name to fill a blank spot that arises on the couch, they will know which players are holding boys' names and which are holding girls' names and call accordingly. Players are not allowed to give hints to each other.

Grab and Guess

Give each person a pencil and sheet of paper numbered one through thirty. Behind a blanket hung up to form a curtain, position a player holding a bag that contains the items listed below. That person will take one item out at a time and allow the rest of the group to take turns (five seconds only) touching the object with their hands. (Players can reach around a narrow blanket to touch the object, or if you pick up a thrift-shop blanket you could make two slits in it for players to reach their hands through.) No one, however, is allowed to see the items behind the curtain. After each object is touched, players return to their seats and write down what they think the object is. The player with the most correct guesses wins.

1. flashcube
2. dime
3. key
4. glass
5. coffee strainer
6. pen
7. cassette tape
8. crayon
9. paper clip
10. spoon
11. stuffed animal
12. guitar pick
13. comb
14. envelope
15. rubber band
16. Band-Aid
17. spool of thread
18. postage stamp
19. billiard chalk
20. calculator
21. light bulb

22. bobby pin	25. flashlight battery	28. bagel
23. safety pin	26. clock or watch	29. thimble
24. extension cord	27. toy car	30. cotton ball

Guess the Object

Whether your group's large or small, this living-room game is fun. Tell the group that five volunteers will leave the room while the remainder of the group chooses an object for the volunteers to guess when they return. Once the volunteers are out of the room, however, give the real rules of the game.

Rather than choosing an object, the group will respond to the volunteer according to a set of conditions like the following: If a volunteer guesses any object whose name ends with F, the group will say, "More specific." If the name of the object guessed begins with F, the group responds in unison, "Yes!" If the guess neither begins nor ends with F, the group response is "No!"

When the conditions for that round have been explained, one of the five people comes back into the room and is told to guess what the object is. The group responds in unison according to the conditions explained earlier. The volunteer continues guessing until the group responds, "Yes!" At this point the game is explained to the volunteer and a new set of conditions is announced for the next volunteer.

Hang It on Your Beak! *6/00 Staff*

With only a package of plastic teaspoons and a little practice, you'll break up your crowd in no time! First (at home), practice hanging a spoon on your nose. You'll have to rub the oil off your nose with your shirt sleeve, breathe heavily on the inside of the spoon, then hang it on the end of your nose.

After you teach your crowd this, uh, trick, then start some competition:
  • See who can hang the spoon off his or her schnozz the longest.

- See how many players can get the spoon off the ends of their noses and into their mouths—using only their tongues.
- See how many players can hang a spoon off any part of their faces or arms.

Award comic prizes to the winners. Bring along some spoons of varying sizes and styles to let the kids try them on for size.

High Roller, High Writer

Get a small group of kids around a table, and place in the middle one die and one pencil. Provide a sheet of paper for each player. Determine who plays first, then begin: the first player rolls the die once, then passes it clockwise so the next player can also roll once before passing the die on.

When a player rolls a six, he or she grabs the pencil and begins writing from 1 to 100—1,2,3,4,5, and so on.

Meanwhile, the die is passed from player to player as before, each trying to roll a six. The writers goal is to reach 100 before another player rolls a six, grabs the pencil from the first writer, and starts furiously scribbling numbers. Speed, of course, is the essence with both the number-writing and die-rolling—and the intensity builds as players get closer and closer to 100 before they're robbed of the pencil. First player to reach 100 wins.

License Plates

Here's a take-off on a game most folks have played while traveling in a car. List on a blackboard, overhead, or handout the following state nicknames (and others you may know) from auto license plates. Then have your group divide up into teams to identify the correct state for each name. The team that correctly identifies the most states wins the game. You can play the game several times by only using ten states at a time. If the game seems too difficult for your age group, provide the state names as well (out of order) and make it a matching game.

First in Flight	North Carolina
The Empire State	New York
The Aloha State	Hawaii
The Grand Canyon State	Arizona
The Keystone State	Pennsylvania
Land of Opportunity	Arkansas
The Vacation State	Maine
The Centennial State	Colorado
The Volunteer State	Tennessee
The Constitution State	Connecticut
The Land of Enchantment	New Mexico
First State	Delaware
The Golden State	California
The Hoosier State	Indiana
The Sportsman's State	Louisiana
The Hawkeye State	Iowa
Land of Lincoln	Illinois
The Sunflower State	Kansas
The Great Lake State	Michigan
The Bluegrass State	Kentucky
The Silver State	Nevada
The Bay State	Massachusetts
Land of 10,000 Lakes	Minnesota
The Magnolia State	Mississippi
The Show-me State	Missouri
The Ocean State	Rhode Island
The Garden State	New Jersey
The Lone Star State	Texas
The Peach State	Georgia
The Heart of Dixie	Alabama
The Sunshine State	Florida
America's Dairyland	Wisconsin

Locker Lotto

This back-to-school relay can be used to introduce your topic—especially one relating to school and stress.

Before the game, write out a key word that relates to your study (pressure, homework, term papers), one letter per sheet. Make as many copies of the word as there will be teams. At the bottom of each sheet, write a different set of three numbers that suggest a locker combination—9-3-5, for example. Crumple each sheet into a ball, and put a word's worth of "lotto balls" in as many bags or boxes as there will be teams.

The relay runs like this: the first members of each team must pull a lotto ball from the bag, "open the locker" by spinning themselves per their "combination" (that is, nine times around to the left and three times around to the right, five more times to the left), then stagger back to their teams to add their letter to the mystery word. The team that unscrambles the letters to guess the word correctly wins.

Movie Madness

6|00 Stuff

Distribute one 3 x 5 card to each teenager and instruct all players to write down the name of a movie, TV program, or commercial. Players should not see what each other has written. Collect the cards.

Now divide the group into teams of four or five (involve the adult sponsors, too) and have each team draw one card from the pile you're holding. Teams then take three to five minutes to quickly plan a scene from the movie, TV program, or commercial they chose. After you've gathered the groups together again, let the teams act out their scenes one at a time. The other teams can guess what movie, program, or commercial the performing team is portraying only when the performing team is finished.

For extra fun, record the evening on video—then edit it and play it at your next movie night.

Personality Pursuit

Before you play this game, have 200 - 300 small strips of paper prepared. When the group arrives, have them write on each strip a person's name—use the name of others in your group, or celebrities' names, names of people dead or alive, comic strip characters—just as long as the name is well-known to most of the group. Don't worry if names are written more than once—it makes the game more fun. Then put all these strips in a pail or box.

Now divide into two teams. A player from team A dips into the pail, grabs a name, and has thirty seconds to give clues to his teammates until they can guess the name. Any verbal clue is permissible—even pointing is allowed. If his team guesses the name within thirty seconds, that strip is pocketed by the team for scoring later; if the team fails to guess the name, the strip goes back into the bucket. Then team B follows suit. Make sure clue-givers are rotated each turn.

At the end of a designated time, each team tallies up the names the members have correctly guessed, and the team with the most wins.

Pigskins and Pucks

Time to put all your sports-spectating prowess to work. The object of the two quizzes ("Touchdown!" and "On Ice") is to identify the football teams and the hockey teams from the clues. Prepare the quizzes and pass them out to your group for some fun during the halftime of a TV game they're watching. (See the quiz clues on the next page)

Here are the quiz clues:

Touchdown!

Can you recall which NFL teams go with the following clues?

1. Ranch hands
2. Cherokee, Navajo, Blackfoot, etc.
3. Bald birds
4. Catholic officials
5. Goliaths
6. Eric the Red's crew
7. Koala, grizzly, panda
8. Suitcase stuffers
9. Kings of the beasts
10. Pirates
11. Gold diggers
12. Holy ones
13. Swift birds of prey
14. Head bashers
15. Small whales
16. Young horses
17. Minutemen
18. F-15s
19. William Cody namesakes
20. Ironmen
21. Fossil drillers
22. Earth colors
23. India's cats
24. Vandals
25. Rodeo mounts
26. Aquatic fliers
27. Indian leaders
28. The electric company

On Ice

Come on, all you hockey jocks. See how many NHL teams you can name from these clues. And remember—no high-sticking!

1. Birds in tuxedos
2. These big ones available at Burger King
3. These are "lite" swords
4. The compass always points to these satellites
5. Fast airplanes
6. Frequent ones receive bonus mileage
7. These guys are from the Great White North
8. Embarrassed parts of a bird
9. On fire and all ablaze
10. "You got me singing the —"

11. Remote inhabitants, much like Gilligan
12. Forest Police
13. Falling from a syrupy tree
14. Well-drilled wells, not for water
15. Name of the bear in Reynard the Fox
16. A native of northern Europe
17. Ten, jack, queen, king...
18. This is a great kind of idea
19. French Canadian or Canadian French
20. A dark bird of prey
21. The fallen angel

Here are the answers:

Touchdown!

1. Dallas Cowboys
2. Washington Redskins
3. Philadelphia Eagles
4. Phoenix Cardinals
5. New York Giants
6. Minnesota Vikings
7. Chicago Bears
8. Green Bay Packers
9. Detroit Lions
10. Tampa Bay Buccaneers
11. San Francisco 49ers
12. New Orleans Saints
13. Atlanta Falcons
14. Los Angeles Rams
15. Miami Dolphins
16. Indianapolis Colts
17. New England Patriots
18. New York Jets
19. Buffalo Bills
20. Pittsburgh Steelers
21. Houston Oilers
22. Cleveland Browns
23. Cincinnati Bengals
24. Los Angeles Raiders
25. Denver Broncos
26. Seattle Seahawkes
27. Kansas City Chiefs
28. San Diego Chargers

On Ice

1. Pittsburgh Penguins
2. Hartford Whalers
3. Buffalo Sabres
4. Minnesota North Stars
5. Winnipeg Jets
6. Philadelphia Flyers
7. Montreal Canadians
8. Detroit Red Wings
9. Calgary Flames
10. St. Louis Blues
11. New York Islanders
12. New York Rangers
13. Toronto Maple Leafs
14. Edmonton Oilers
15. Boston Bruins
16. Quebec Nordiques
17. Los Angeles Kings
18. Washington Capitols
19. Vancouver Canucks
20. Chicago Blackhawkes
21. New Jersey Devils

Up Jenkins

This game of concealment and feint is best played by small, even groups of six to twelve players. All that's needed is a long table, chairs for all players, and a quarter. Divide people into two teams; teams sit on opposite sides of the table. Each team selects a captain.

The game begins with one team secretly passing the quarter back and forth among themselves underneath the table. When the captain of the opposing team says "Up Jenkins!" all the players on the quarter-passing team close their fists, lift their arms, and place their elbows on the table. In one of the fists, of course, is the quarter. Then the opposing captain says, "Down Jenkins!" and all the players simultaneously slam their hands down on the table. If it's done well, the other team won't be able to hear the quarter.

The object then is for the guessing team to eliminate all the hands that do not have the quarter, leaving at last the one hand with the quarter under it. So the opposing captain chooses people to lift a hand, one hand at a time. The team with the quarter can respond to the captain only; lifting a hand in response to anyone else on the opposing team means forfeiture of the quarter. One of the goals of the opposing team, therefore, is to persuade people to lift their hands in response to someone other than its captain. If the opposing team's captain successfully lifts all the hands except the one covering the quarter, his or her team wins and takes possession of the quarter. If, however, the captain uncovers the quarter before the last hand, the quarter-passing team retains possession and another round begins.

Once the kids get the hang of it, they'll develop all sorts of strategies—how to make your hand "look guilty" when you don't have the quarter, and so on.

Words

The imaginations, vocabulary, and teamwork of your youth group will get a workout with this one. Give each team a list with several combinations in it - PMR, for example, and CRY and SPF. Each team attempts to make a word that keeps the letters in their order. From PMR a team might make **ProMpteR**; from CRY, un**CleaRlY**. The team with the longest word wins that round—un**CleaRlY**, for example, beats **CRY**ing.

The winner of the most rounds wins the game. Variations? Require that words be proper nouns, foreign words, biblical words.

INDEX

This is the complete list of game titles for *Play It Again!* alphabetically organized without regard for the chapters in which the games appear.